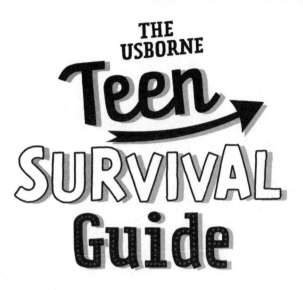

THE USBORNE Teen SURVIVAL Guide

Caroline Young

Designed by
Stephanie Jeffries

Illustrated by
The Boy Fitz Hammond
and Laura Wood

Edited by
Felicity Brooks

Usborne Quicklinks

The internet is a great source of information, but it's very important to know which sites you can trust.

We have selected some useful websites to supplement the information in this book and these are available at **Usborne Quicklinks**. Here you can find more advice about healthy eating, sexuality, bullying, social media and lots, lots more.

For links to all these sites, go to:

usborne.com/Quicklinks

and type in the title of this book
or scan the QR code above.

Please follow the internet safety guidelines at
Usborne Quicklinks. Children should be supervised online.

Introduction

Your teenage years are a time of change in almost every area of your life. Your body will begin to change, slowly becoming the adult version of you. Your daily life will change, as school pressures intensify and you begin to think about what comes *after* school. Your feelings about yourself, other people and the world change enormously too, as you learn more and think more deeply about what matters to you.

All this makes these years especially important, but it doesn't always make them easy. This book looks at some of the issues that can affect teenagers as they grow and develop, and offers loads of useful advice for getting you through them. There will be bumps in the road, but this book aims to be a celebration of this amazing time in your life, and to help you see just how special you are.

Contents

This explains some of the terms used in this book. The first time you see any glossary words or phrases, they'll look like **this**.

Chapter One

Being the best you can be

As a teenager, you'll know that life is much more fun if you're feeling good about yourself. You're more likely to feel this way when you are a) happy and b) healthy, but these two words can mean different things to different people. At times, it can feel like a lot of pressure to be...

As a young person, you might feel adults give you a hard time. They might call you 'irritable', 'irritating', 'irrational' or 'irresponsible' (lots of 'irr' words, basically). This is tough to hear. Try to remember that, in many ways, your age is a **fantastic** one. You have passion and potential that others don't. You've got a brain primed to learn 24/7*. Your body has loads of energy and your imagination is in overdrive. You are finding out who you are, and who you'll become, which is a pretty important thing to be doing.

There are plenty of books for adults, advising them how to cope with teens, but...

this book is for <u>YOU</u>.

It's packed full of ideas, tips and information to help you live the happiest, healthiest life you can, but still be a) sane and b) yourself.

*It might surprise you to learn that your teenage brain is able to learn more, and remember more, than it will for the rest of your life. Go you!

First, let's look at happiness

So, what is it? Well, for some people, happiness is skateboarding. For others, it's playing a guitar and for others, it's dancing until dawn.

Every one of us is unique, so there is no single, fail-safe recipe: you need to find what makes YOU happy... and that may take a bit of thinking about.

Next, **health...**

Being happy is closely tied up with being healthy. If your physical health isn't good (because you're ill) you're probably not very happy, either. The same applies if your **mental health*** is not good (because you're sad or anxious). You don't feel good at all, do you?

These headaches are getting worse and worse. I'm soooo fed-up.

Both together

Yes, health and happiness are so closely linked that you need to think about them as equally important parts of the whole of YOU. This means you need to take care of both of them.

*Words and phrases you may need to look up, that are underlined like **this**, are explained in the Glossary on pages 273–276.

It can be easy to think that everything in your life will be wonderful when you:

Get that new jacket	✓
Reach a thousand followers online	✓
Pass the next test	✓

It's even easier to think that life would be fine if you:

Won the lottery	✓
Invented something incredibly useful	✓
Inherited a fortune from an unknown distant relative	◯

But research shows that even big things like this don't affect what's called your 'baseline happiness' for very long. You might feel a bit happier, and buy lots of stuff, but after a while, you'll feel just like you did before.

That's news to me!

It's true that if, say, you've been unhappy with your hairstyle and have a new one, you might feel great... until, perhaps, the next niggling worry comes into your head.

Being happy and healthy is more of an ongoing journey than a specific destination (clichéd as that sounds). We are all in this for the long haul, but as you develop, learn and change, what matters to you and what makes you happy will probably change a lot too.

Put simply, being happy and healthy in life depends mainly on these three things:

> liking and accepting yourself

> taking care of yourself

> feeling fulfilled and loved

I feel safe

Sound good? Well, this book is a realistic, useful and practical guide to help you achieve those things, and more. See it as a survival kit for your amazing teenage years... and read on.

How well do you really know yourself?

The answer to that question is 'probably not as well as you think you do'. But to survive these teenage years as well as possible, getting to know yourself better is a really good start.

So, what kind of person do you think you are? Here are some of the words you might use to describe yourself, but there are many more. If you had to choose **just three** of them, which ones would you go for?

I am...

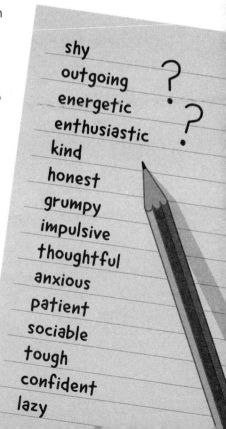

shy
outgoing
energetic
enthusiastic
kind
honest
grumpy
impulsive
thoughtful
anxious
patient
sociable
tough
confident
lazy

If you found that tricky, don't worry.

It was supposed to be.

Each person is the result of lots of different experiences, influences, thoughts and feelings. People can sometimes be shy with strangers, but outgoing with family and friends, or lazy if they don't want to do the dishes and energetic when they play football. This is made even **more** complicated when other people 'label' us, judge us, **stereotype** us or say we're something we know we're not. That can hurt.

MACHO

LAZY TOUGH

I'm so much more than they think I am.

So, let's forget what anyone else thinks and focus on helping you get to know yourself, because you're uniquely, wonderfully GREAT!

The same, but different

All the people on Earth have a LOT in common: we all have a brain, and we all bleed if we're hurt, for example. But we are unique in so many other ways: the *exact* colour of our hair, our voice and our sense of humour, for instance.

Human beings are complex and you're going through probably the most turbulent time of your life. Chemicals called **hormones** are zooming around your body and they can seriously affect your moods. But if you feel your body's changing a lot,* you'll be amazed at what's going on in your brain!

*You can read more about these physical changes in Chapter 13.

How do you feel?

Your incredible brain changes more during the years between the ages of 11 and your early twenties than at any other time, and these changes have a HUGE impact on how you feel, think and react to things.

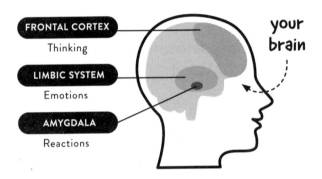

Every part of the brain that you see here has a different job, but a teenage brain is very highly-developed in one area, called the **amygdala**.* It's very small, but it is VERY important. What it does might explain a lot about how young people feel and behave.

*The word 'amygdala' is from the Greek word for almond, 'amygdale'. That's how small it is!

Your amygdala is a bit like a control centre for:

- **Your emotions, how you react to things and people around you.**
- **How you respond to any stress or difficulty you encounter.**
- **Impulses and temptations — and whether you take unwise risks.**

And last of all, it can make you feel *embarrassed* more easily, more of the time. Some people describe an 'imaginary audience', that follows young people wherever they go, judging them. How stressful is that?

23

Blame your brain

To a large extent, you can blame your brain for the fact that, during these vital years of growth and change, it's very easy to:

* Lose your temper with people.
* Assume the worst in a situation.
* Blame yourself when things go wrong.

* Think about yourself, your appearance and your problems 24/7.
* Do silly things you really wish you hadn't.
* Not be able to 'read the room', and react appropriately.
* Try new things without thinking them through (or 'novelty-seeking').

This is all understandable, natural behaviour for you, but it can cause a lot of

#!@$!!

arguments

SLAMMED DOORS

detentions

and *general misery*

Before you think it's fine to keep doing all this stuff because it's your brain's fault, remember that there's nearly always a choice.

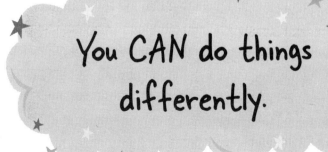

You CAN do things differently.

What would you do?

Let's think about how you might respond to these potentially tricky situations. There isn't a 'right' answer, but you'll see that there are definitely better, wiser ones. Don't overthink it, but do be honest in your choices. Remember, no one will know your answers.

Q1: At the last minute, a mate has asked another friend to go fishing this Saturday instead of you. You were really looking forward to it. Do you:

a) Fire off an angry message, saying just how let down you feel and telling them you aren't their mate anymore.

b) Tell them that you feel disappointed and think they could have given you more notice.

c) Don't reply at all, because it's probably something you said or did that's made them change their mind.

Phew! That's me off the hook.

Q2: A teacher has set a big assignment. If you do it, you won't have time to go to the gig this weekend. Do you:

a)   Storm out of the lesson and refuse to do the assignment. Getting a detention will be worth it.

b)   Calmly explain the situation to the teacher, do what you can in the time you have but ask for some flexibility on the deadline.

c)   Resign yourself to a weekend working. You probably wouldn't have enjoyed the gig anyway, knowing you.

Q3: Some of your friends have started missing lessons. They want you to join them, because 'it's a laugh', but you all have exams soon. Do you:

a)   Tell your friends that you think they're idiots and that you're going to tell a teacher.

b)   Say that you'd rather do the lessons, hang out with them after school and plan some serious fun for after the exams.

c)   Go with them, because if you don't, you'll have no mates and NO lesson is worth that much grief.

Turn the page to see what your answers reveal...

So which ones did you choose?

If you chose the **a)** answers, you're
letting your emotions decide what
you do, and reacting almost without
thinking (even if what happens next
is not good).

If you chose the **b)** answers, well done.
You stopped, thought, and reacted
wisely, without making things more
stressful for anyone.

If you chose the **c)** answers, imagine
how you would you feel afterwards.
Would you be happier, or would you
feel even worse?

Two minds? Who knew?

It can be easy – especially with that amygdala in overdrive – to react without thinking. Experts often call this letting your 'emotional mind' take control of your 'wise mind'. If you can, take a deep breath and wait a while before responding to situations that could go wrong. Then try these tips:

count to ten

focus on something solid in the room

imagine the fallout if you explode

think calm thoughts

OK, breathe. 1... 2...

You'll probably find you feel much happier and have fewer arguments if you can control your reactions a little more. It takes practice, but you can do it.

SPLAT

What do I do?

As well as trying to understand your emotions, research shows that everyone needs to **do** a variety of things to enjoy life more. Here are some things that experts recommend doing to increase happiness levels:

A Something that gets you moving

WOOF WOOF

B An activity that includes other people

Mix and match

Some of these activities tick several 'happiness' boxes, which is great. It's time to think about what you do each week, and what makes you happy. Turn the page to see more.

Happiness log

Every day for a week, if you do one of these things, jot it down. Label them A, B, C or D, based on the 'types of happiness' on the previous page. Here are some possibilities:

My happiness log

A+B+C+D

MONDAY
tried a new dance class after school

TUESDAY
chatted to Gran and Grandad — B

WEDNESDAY
started reading a really good book
— C

THURSDAY
made pasta and sauce for tea —
C

FRIDAY
met some mates in town — B

SATURDAY
watched a movie with Dan and Esme
— B+D

SUNDAY
played football — A+B

Did you find you had something to add to your list for every day of the week? If you did, that's great. You're already doing things that will form a key part of your happiness mix, but if you didn't, don't worry. Help is at hand...

What do I enjoy?

If your 'list of happy things' wasn't a long one, think about what you *enjoy* doing. If these are good, positive activities for you, whatever they are, that's fine. Could you do more of them, or even try something new? Research shows that doing something completely new, or trying to master a new skill, can make you feel good, and certainly perks up that mega-brain of yours.

I never thought I'd enjoy baking so much.

What DON'T I enjoy?

Another way of boosting your happiness levels is to take a close look at what you're doing that you *don't* enjoy. This could be something like:

> Arguing with my family, and not saying sorry even when I know I'm in the wrong.

> Spending longer than you'd like to scrolling on your phone.

Yes, you!

> Hanging out with people you don't really like.

Being *aware* of things like this in your life means you can make a change and build in more of the things that DO make you happy.

P.S.

Sorry, but some things in life just HAVE to be done, whether they make you feel good or not. These might include homework and taking the bins out.

What matters to me?

The final part of building a kind of 'profile' of yourself is to think about the things that really matter to you. They are a vital part of your happiness and go deeper than quick fixes like a new school bag or getting 100 likes on a post (good as those can feel!). Here are some examples to help you think, but yours will probably be just as unique as you are:

trying hard at school

staying fit and healthy

my mum, stepdad and stepbrothers

getting outside in the fresh air every day

Ali and Ciara

being kind

Hey, these things really do matter to me.

There are many, many more things you could choose, of course. Jot down a list of yours, and then put a number next to each one to rate them in order of importance. If 'friends' mean the most to you, for example, you'll put a '1' next to that in your list.

Feeling comfy and relaxed might be on your list.

You'll be looking at this list again as you read this book, as these things are at the heart of who you are and how good you feel about life. They may change as you change, but they matter to you here and now and they are a great start on your journey to becoming the person you want to be and surviving these turbulent teenage years.

Chapter Three

How much do you LIKE yourself?

This chapter looks at how much you like being YOU, which has a big impact on how you feel, and live your life. Hopefully, you feel that you're a pretty sound person, but if you're not so sure, don't panic. At times, it's not easy to like ourselves, but there are lots of suggestions coming up to help you start to see yourself in a more positive way (as everyone else probably sees you already...).

Self-esteem

Put simply, **self-esteem** means

having value and respect for yourself.

Sounds good, doesn't it? And it *is*. We all need to value and respect ourselves, because if we don't, other people might not value or respect us either, which can make life pretty grim.

You may not feel that your self-esteem is sky high right now. It's much easier to see what you *don't* like about yourself than what you *do*. Luckily, your super-agile teenage brain is your best ally, as it can learn new ways of thinking which will help you challenge those negative thoughts and have better ones.

I've got this.

Being perfect

Few people feel totally happy with themselves 24/7. Even rich, uber-groomed celebrities have insecurities, and have to work VERY HARD to keep up their perfect/buff/happy image. It's a full-time job.

I hope I look good enough for the red carpet.

But there are ways you can a) value yourself more and b) accept the things you can't change about yourself. In small, simple ways, they can all help you feel better in yourself (and let you have a life as well). Win-win.

Three good things about me

Let's start with some positivity. Jot down three things about yourself that you LIKE, or think are good. (For now, don't focus on your physical appearance.) They might be:

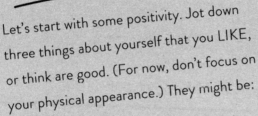

1) I am kind to other people.
2) I am good at playing basketball.
3) I write interesting stories.

Three not-so-good things

If you found that tricky, this will probably be easier. Jot down three things you DON'T LIKE about yourself. Again, don't focus on your appearance. Something like this, perhaps:

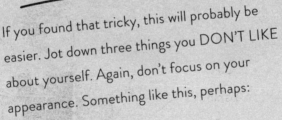

1) I am always late, for everything.
2) I never score a goal in hockey.
3) I am the worst in the class at algebra.

Now read your list out loud, and really *listen* to the words. Be honest: did you find things like:

Well, perhaps not 'never'

or

Not yet, but I will

creeping into your head? If you did, well done. If you didn't, take note...

It's very easy to criticize yourself, but it's very important to learn to *defend* yourself from criticism as well. Being positive, rather than negative, about yourself is a skill you can learn,* but you may need to practise it a bit.

I know I don't sound so good now, but I'm definitely getting better.

THE NOISE

*You'll find some tips on pages 47–49.

Liking my body

For most young people, their self-esteem is very focused on appearance. Your clothes, hair, skin and overall 'look' are important, because they are part of who you are and how you want the world to see you, but let's think about what's underneath it all – your *body*. How much do you like yours?

OK, you might find what's coming next
a bit uncomfortable, but do your best.
(Oh, and you don't need to be naked, btw!)

1 Stand in front of a mirror,
facing forward.

2 Take a good, long look at
yourself, from top to toe.

3 Say three things you LIKE
about your body, out loud.
(Or whisper them if you
find that easier.)

Did you manage three? Well done if so, because
many, many people can't do that, which is sad.

Next, follow steps 1 and 2 again. Now, say three
things you DISLIKE about your body out loud.

Did you find that easier? Yup, that **critical voice** inside your head is *so much louder*, always happily pointing out all your shortcomings and not celebrating your good qualities. But you can begin to change that right now. Read on...

Change the channel

Always seeing and saying negative things about yourself is like having a radio on in the background of your life telling you you're rubbish, or not good enough. If this is you, perhaps it's time to change the channel (if you find turning it off altogether too tough).

This tip might help:

From now on, whenever you feel something negative about yourself popping into your head, fight back with something positive. Turning off all the negativity you feel about yourself can make a big difference. For example:

I always forget to put my clean washing away.

BUT

I always thank the person who washed it for me.

or perhaps...

I never change the loo roll when it runs out.

BUT

I never leave my wet towel on the bathroom floor.

The more you do this, the easier it gets. Another tip is to imagine someone was saying something really unkind to a friend. What would you say, to make them feel better about themselves? Well, say that to yourself, RIGHT NOW!

I'm OK, actually

Here are lots more tips to help you think more positively about yourself, and about your life. Try them out a few times and they'll get easier:

1 **Beware of using the words 'always', 'worst' or 'never' about yourself**

Your *thought* is not a *fact*, remember.

2 **Notice when you put yourself down, or don't value yourself**

Try to do things differently, and more positively, next time.

3 **Be kind to yourself**

In your head, say positive things like "I'm OK", or "I'm just as good as anyone else in this room".

I deserve this.

4 Keep it in perspective

Ask yourself how much will all this matter in an hour, a day, a week, a month. Probably not much, right?

5 Let it go

Relax, and imagine those negative feelings washing over you, and then flowing past, and away.

Body positivity

There is a powerful 'movement' at the moment to help people *accept* their bodies, whatever their size and shape. Some celebrities have helped spread this message, especially to young people. It's called **body positivity**, and, overall, it's a VERY good thing.

I love my body!

It's great to embrace who you are and feel you're worth valuing, because you ARE, but you need to remember that liking and respecting your body includes looking after it.

You'll find lots more about how to keep your body fit and healthy in Chapters 6 and 7 of this book.

This is me

Have you ever thought
what the words 'perfect' or
'beautiful' actually mean?
What one person finds totally
gorgeous, another might
not. You are SO much more
than what you look like, or
your body shape, however
important both of these
might seem at the moment.

Ah, such perfection.

Remember those 'things that really matter to
me' that you listed in Chapter 2? They make
you *you*, and the people who love you know that.
Sticking to those values in everything you do will
boost your self-esteem more than any make-up
or make-over. You are YOU, a real, unfiltered,
unique and wonderful person. In fact, **you are
like nobody else, anywhere,** so celebrate it!

How much do you like yourself *now*?

Choose one answer to these questions. Answer honestly, remembering all the info in this chapter:

Q1: You are in town with a mate, trying on clothes. They've bought loads of stuff but you can't find anything you like. How do you feel?

a) Gutted. It's not fair that you can never find anything that fits, or looks good. Another wasted weekend.

b) A bit disappointed, but there are plenty of other shops to try. You don't really share your mate's taste anyway.

c) Decide to shop online. Then, nobody can see you if you look terrible in everything, as usual.

Q2: In PE lessons, you dread it if teams need to be picked in case you're the last one to get chosen, or don't get chosen at all. How do you feel when it happens?

a) You put up with it, but feel terrible if you get left until last because everyone thinks you're rubbish. Perhaps they are right, and you ARE.

b) You try to feel proud of keeping on going. Everyone else probably feels anxious and self-conscious too, even if they don't show it.

c) You bring a sick note as often as you can, so that you can skip the lessons. It's worth missing out on the exercise to avoid feeling bad.

Q3: **You and your best friend follow an influencer, and your friend has started trying to look like them. They want you to join in. What do you do?**

a) Tell your friend straight that you can't afford it and think it's all a bit silly. They can never look like that, however much they spend.

b) Kindly explain that, although you like reading the influencer's posts, you're quite happy with your own 'look'.

c) Agree to join in and try to copy the style you both want to achieve as closely as you can. It will be worth the time and money to look like that.

Q4: **You have really wanted to change your hairstyle for ages, but know some of your mates or family won't approve if you do. Do you:**

a) Keep the same hairstyle as most people have. Being left out is not worth it.

b) Go for it, and hold your head up high! Not everyone can like everything.

c) Try to change your mates' minds. If you can't, doing nothing is safer.

Turn the page to see what your answers reveal...

What do my answers mean?

As usual in this book, none of these answers is wrong, but the **b)** answers show the highest level of 'respect and value for yourself', or self-esteem.

If you didn't choose them, think about whether you could have done, and how you would feel if you had.

If you chose the **a)** and **c)** answers, they are negative choices that don't let you be your true self or acknowledge your feelings.

Chapter Four

Families, and how to survive them

So you've seen that being a teen can be a pretty eventful time, not just for you, but for those close to you. Whatever kind of family or carers you have, you'll spend a LOT of time with them during your lifetime – some experts reckon an average of 25,000 hours from babyhood to when you reach adulthood, in fact.

Do you remember that your brain is developing and changing all the time, making it hard for you to control your reactions to what people do or say? Yup, you're often '**hypertense**', which can lead to clashes with anyone within range. As this is frequently your family, things can get tricky...

Forgive and forget

Yes, it's a shame, but quarrels are a normal, natural part of you beginning to separate yourself from the people you live with (a.k.a *growing up!*). To be honest, it's probably a good idea to accept that they are going to happen from time to time, *whatever any of you do*. The hope to hold onto is that people who care about you will understand, forgive you and forget the really horrible things you just yelled at them. It's a big ask, but most families do in the end. Honestly.

People need people

All the research into happiness shows that we all need other people to be happy. This means it's worth investing time and effort in relationships with those closest to you, however challenging that may seem. This chapter is full of tips to help you do that.

Does one-size-fit-all?

No, not really. Just as there are many different kinds of family, there are many different kinds of parents and carers too. Ideally, whoever is caring for you should:

- Listen to you and respect your opinions
- Be interested in what you're doing
- Reassure and calm you if you're stressed
- Offer advice and guidance
- Give you time and space to be yourself

Daily life is full of challenges, however, and different parents/carers react to them in different ways. It might be worth trying to see things from *their* point of view from time to time, tricky as that can be, remembering that they have their own problems too. Family life is constant give and take, so you might need to do a little more giving. Just sayin'.

So much to do...

Can I give you a hand?

HOME SURVIVAL TIPS

1 Talk to each other

The simplest way of making sure your parents/carers know what's going on in your life is to TELL THEM. They can't see inside your head to know that, say, school is rubbish at the moment or a friend was unkind. This may feel awkward at first, but once you start, it will get easier. If they don't know, they can't help, so talk to them.

I'm freaking out! I don't understand this topic at ALL.

I'm absolutely fine!

② You could do something fun together

Spend some relaxed, easy time with your family. Watch a boxset, play a game, cook a meal together or go for a walk. Such simple things can renew the bond between you all, without having to spend much or even feel pressured to chat if you don't want to.

❸ Be calm and clear

It can be easy to blurt things out angrily, without thinking, especially at home. Try the simple tips on page 29 to give yourself a few seconds' leeway. This may be all you need to diffuse tension and be able to talk things through calmly and clearly. It may not always work, but if you make it a habit, you might find that there are at least fewer arguments/slammed doors.

❹ Try to see each other's viewpoint

This is not always easy. In fact, it can be VERY DIFFICULT, but trying to understand *why* the other person feels as they do (and not the same as you) is worthwhile. Give them time and space to explain their viewpoint to you, and make sure you get the chance to do the same to them. You'll learn to understand each other better and get through tricky times together.

❺ Respect each other

A lot of young people feel the adults in their life don't respect or understand them, but every adult was a teen once, however different the world was then. Could you, gently, remind them of that fact from time to time? And finally, of course, respect is **earned**: if you show your family some, they are more likely to do the same to you.

❻ Remember they CARE

Your parents/carers are probably doing their best to make your home a happy one (though it may not feel like it sometimes). These stormy days will pass, so try not to expect perfection from each other. If you can, remember that your parents or carers love you, worry about you and want you to be happy. They also often PAY FOR STUFF!

Bigger problems

The advice in this chapter centres on trying to support, understand and respect your family, but there are times when stuff in the adults' lives needs to be left to them. These might include divorce, serious illness or financial pressures.

If these problems arise, it's important to remember that **they are not your fault, and you are not responsible for solving them**.

You have the right to live your own life, and focus on the things that matter to you and will influence your future. If you feel in the middle of problems or conflict at home, make sure you talk to your mates, teachers, and, perhaps, your siblings, and let your feelings out. It's not your role to make things better for everyone around you. Focus on your needs first: you owe that to yourself.

What would you do?

Here are some tricky situations that might arise at home from time to time. Be completely honest, and choose one answer to each question.

Q1: You want to go to a party on Saturday night, but your dad isn't keen. How do you react?

    a)   Tell him that everyone else is going, and he really needs to loosen up a bit.

    b)   Talk it through with him, to see if you can reassure him that it will be fine, and you'll be sensible.

    c)   Lose your cool, and tell him that you are going to go whatever he says. And slam the door.

Q2: You really want to go on the school trip, but it's expensive. How do you put it to your parents/carers?

    a)   Tell them that you'll be the ONLY one not going which will make you (and them) look like losers.

    b)   Offer to do lots of jobs for them, and say you'll contribute to the cost if they agree.

    c)   Tell them straight that you need to go, end of. Remind them of all the things THEY spend cash on to have fun.

Q3: You're stressed about an exam that's coming up. How do you behave at home?

a) Give your parents/carers a wide berth until it's over. They won't understand anyway.

b) Explain how you're feeling, and apologize if you're a bit bad-tempered around the place at the moment.

c) Tell everyone to leave you alone at all times to concentrate on this VERY IMPORTANT exam.

Q4: You're feeling overloaded with too many after school activities. What would you do?

Not sure I can keep all this up.

a) Just don't go to the ones you don't feel like going to. Problem solved.

b) Ask your parents/carers to help you prioritize what you do after school, as it's all getting a bit much.

c) Drop some of the activities, and tell them after you've done so. You have to come first.

Turn the page to see what your answers reveal...

What do my answers mean?

Whatever answers you chose, none of them is 'right', but if you chose the **b)** answers, well done. You are including your parents or carers in your life in a calm, mature way, which is great. You may not always agree with their decisions, and there may be religious or cultural traditions and beliefs in the mix, but that's life, really.

Try to remember that, like you, adults have their own worries and concerns, and can only do their best. You didn't arrive with a manual, so they are learning on the job! BUT there are ways of making life a little happier at home if you all **communicate.**

Chapter Five

Friendships, and how to survive them

For young people, friends are important ingredients in the 'happiness mix'. You might even feel they are more important to you than your family, and understand you soooo much better. (That's actually completely normal, so don't feel bad if this is you.)

BUT, because your friends are so important, if you fall out, it can make you very unhappy indeed. Research shows that friendship problems can cause very real distress to many young people. Bad news.

But friends and good friendships can enrich your life like nothing else if you get them right. This chapter looks at how you can make, and keep, those vital friendships working well.

Yay!

71

What makes a good mate?

Have you ever thought about what you look for in a friend? Well, every friendship is different, but the likelihood is that you'll want your mates to have some, if not all, of these qualities:

Thanks!

They're kind

You need friends who will support you through tough times, and be there if you need them.

KEEP OUT

TOP SECRET

You feel they are trustworthy

If you tell a friend a secret, you need to know they will keep it.

You have lots of things in common

It helps if you like at least some of the same things (and jokes) as your mates do.

I'm really sorry!

They show understanding

Good friends accept you just as you are, and usually forgive you if you mess up.

It's OK. It was an accident.

Looking at all those vital qualities, how do *your* mates measure up? If they don't score too well, or you don't feel relaxed and happy in their company, it might be time to find some new ones. **You deserve better, really.**

Be a friend to yourself

In Chapter 2, we looked at how important it is to like yourself, to feel good. It's important to remember that, however fab your friends are, **you can't expect them to be responsible for your happiness 24/7.** You need to be able to cope without them, at least sometimes.

Everyone has their own lives, insecurities and problems; even your bestie *won't* always be worrying about whether your hair looks good today or what you had for breakfast. Sorry. They'll be thinking about their own hair, a movie they saw, or how much revision they need to do.

If you expect the impossible from your friends, you'll always be disappointed. Like any healthy relationship, friendship is about giving **and** taking — getting that balance right is key. Remember to be a loyal friend to *yourself* first and foremost (because at least you can always rely on yourself to show up!).

Being a good friend

Basically, to have good mates, you need to be one yourself. It all boils down to this:

Treat your friends as you would like them to treat you.

So do you? And do you tick all the friendship boxes listed on page 72–73? If not, you can!

To help you be a great mate, here are some of the most important ingredients in a good friendship. They are all based on making your friends feel *valued*, so that – you hope – they will then value you right back.

Listen to your friends first, rather than wade in with your experiences or giving advice straightaway. This shows that you care.

Hi Zee. Not seen you around. R U OK?

Yeah.
...well, no, not really.
I need your help.

Something really weird happened after school.

Tell me everything.
I'm listening :)

...

BUZZ

PING

Thank them from time
to time, for all they do for you.
You could treat them to a milkshake,
or just say, "thanks for being a good mate".

Support them

A kind word can go a very long
way if a mate is struggling.
It will probably make you
feel good, too.

You're doing
great.

CLINK

Do things together

If a mate suggests doing
something new with you, why
not give it a go? This stuff is
the 'glue' of friendship.

This is the
hardest thing
we've tried yet.

I know!

77

Finding your tribe

Sadly, things are not always straightforward when it comes to making friends. Many teens *don't* find it easy, or feel no one really 'gets' them. This can lead to unhappiness, loneliness and self-doubt, which then trigger lots of other kinds of problems.

If this is you, you are far from alone, but the bottom line is that, to make friends, you need to be willing to take the plunge and *try to*.

We all need other people, and **everyone** is worried about being rejected, or things going wrong. But if you don't make the effort to connect with others, you'll never know if things might have gone *right*. The more you try, the easier it gets, and always remember that **nobody in the whole world is like you, or any better than you** (however much you may think that sometimes). So:

Be BRAVE
Be HONEST
Be KIND and

BE YOURSELF

Online friends

Many people find it easier
to make friends online.
It's less exposing, which,
if you're a bit shy, is a big plus.
You might join a group of gamers, for instance,
which makes playing more enjoyable and keeps
you in touch with other people who share your
interest. There can be problems with online
friendships, though, because you don't know
the other person in reality, or face-to-face.
Overall, it's best to be careful and never give
away personal information such as your address.
You can easily be tricked into trusting someone
you *shouldn't*, and probably *wouldn't* trust if you
met them in person.

You'll find more information about online life, social
media and how they can affect you in Chapter 11
and at **Usborne Quicklinks** (see page 4).

When friendships go wrong

There are many ways in which friendships can go wrong, and all of them will probably have a big impact on you. There is no easy cure for the pain this can cause, but know that it will, and does, end and you will survive it. Everybody involved will heal and move on in time.

Sometimes, friendships end without a particular reason or massive argument – they just fizzle out. You may just 'grow apart' from some friends, or not see eye-to-eye on stuff any more. It happens, and it's natural, but it can feel like a big loss at the time, sadly.

81

Think first

Friendships can end for serious reasons, too. Some young people want to experiment with drugs, drinking a lot,* or skipping school, for example, and you may feel pressure to join them but not want to. If this happens to your friendship group, it's tough, because feeling you fit in with your mates is important, but try to *think about* the risks involved before you take them. Look ahead, and imagine how bad things could get later if you did join in.

*There's more about drugs and alcohol at **Usborne Quicklinks**, to help you manage the pressures they can bring.

This pressured situation is tough: in fact, it's a type of **bullying**, and can take many forms. Remember that a real friend, who values you and your friendship, will never force you to do anything you don't want to. Try as hard as you can to stay true to the things that matter to you. (Why not check back at the list you made in Chapter 2 now, to remind yourself?) Respect your amazing brain and body and try to go for smart choices, even if some of your 'friends' don't. **Be your best self, basically.**

Friends – good, bad or in-between?

Now that you've seen that friends and friendships are pretty much at the heart of your happiness, it's time to assess your skills in having, and being, a good friend. Choose one answer for each of these questions:

Q1: Some members of your group are picking on a boy in your class and want you to join in the 'fun'. You don't want to. What do you do?

a) Don't say anything, but don't get involved either. You need to look after yourself first and foremost.

b) Go with the crowd. If everyone else joins in, it's safer for you if you do as well. It's only a bit of banter, after all.

c) Have a word with the others in your group individually. If they refuse to stop, talk to the teacher. It's bullying and it's wrong.

Q2: Someone from your athletics club has invited you to a party. You want to go, but none of your other school friends is invited. Do you:

a) Go to see who else is there, but don't talk to anyone new if they don't talk to you first, and arrange to leave early.

b) Say you're busy. It would be a nightmare to be at a party without your usual gang (however boring you sometimes find them, tbh).

c) Accept the invite, but say that you sometimes feel a bit awkward with lots of new people. Ask if anyone else from athletics is going too.

Q3: You lent a friend your new jacket and they've lost it. You know they can't afford to replace it any time soon. What do you do?

a) Tell them just how furious you are, and how long you had to save up to buy that jacket. Avoid them for a while, too.

b) Insist that they replace the jacket they lost. Their lack of money isn't your problem, and it's only fair that they pay up.

c) Tell them you're upset, but that you know how gutted they must feel. They owe you one in the future!

Turn the page to see what your answers reveal...

What do my answers mean?

Sorry to tell you, but there aren't any 'right' answers to these questions, but if you chose the **a)** answers, you don't seem very focused on making, finding or being a good friend. If you chose **b)** answers, perhaps you need to think about developing your 'friendship skill set' a little. If you went for **c)** answers, go you! Anyone would be glad to be your mate, because you went for kind, mature and FRIENDLY options!

Chapter Six

Eating well and feeling good

What do you *feel* when you think about food?

HUNGRY?

EXCITED?   NOT MUCH?

It might surprise you to know that many people say that food, and eating something they really enjoy, makes a big difference to how good they feel. In fact, research shows that some foods contain chemicals that may actually make us feel happier, and others (once the initial 'sugar rush' wears off) can make us sadder. Yup, food is powerful stuff.

Bananas can make you feel good? Well, I knew that already.

Our bodies need food as 'fuel' of course, so that we can move/think/do what we need to do. If you don't eat enough good food, it's very unlikely that you'll feel great or be living your best life. This chapter will help you make good food choices, so that you take the best care of your body, your brain and yourself.

What do people eat?

TRY OUR
WONDER
DIET

Unfortunately, (no matter what those blogs and adverts tell you) there is no 'one-size-fits-all' **diet** that guarantees that you are a super-healthy human being who never gets ill and always feels ABSOLUTELY AMAZING. Everyone is different, and what we like to eat can be different too.

If you think about it, people around the world grow, cook and eat an incredible variety of food and tasty, new dishes are being created *all the time*. Nothing stays the same for long because tastes change, foodie fashions come and go, or issues arise that affect what we eat, or want to eat.

Many people now eat less meat because intensive animal farming impacts **climate change**.* Others choose to eat some foods, but not others, and their choice may be based on culture or religion, health or just a personal choice. The key to a healthy diet is to make sure that **whatever you eat** is good nourishing stuff.

*You can find out more about the possible effect of food production on the climate at **Usborne Quicklinks**.

Different diets

The word diet usually means 'the things you eat'. Here are the main kinds of diet you may have heard about. (There are many more, but they are not all good for your health, to be honest: who wants to eat only grapefruit?)

vegetarian

I don't eat any meat at all.

vegan

I don't eat anything that comes from animals.

I eat fish, but not meat.

pescatarian

flexitarian

I choose more plant-based foods than meat ones. I'm doing my best for the planet.

dairy-free diet

My diet excludes dairy products such as milk and cheese.

SOY LATTE

gluten-free diet

I need to avoid gluten as it makes me ill.

GLUTEN-FREE CEREAL

Gluten is a protein found in grains such as wheat, rye and barley.

Whatever kind of diet you eat, you need to ensure you are meeting your body's needs and your diet is balanced.*

*There's more information about how to stay healthy if you don't eat certain foods at **Usborne Quicklinks**.

Getting the balance right

But what does the phrase 'a balanced diet' actually *mean*? It looks something like this:

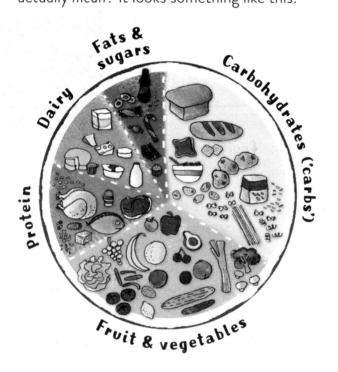

This chart is called **The Eatwell Guide**, and it shows the proportion of each kind of food experts (called dietitians or nutritionists) think you should eat each day.

You don't need to eat everything shown, but roughly that proportion of everything you eat in a day. Ideally, you should aim to eat:

You really DON'T need to eat a mountain of broccoli every day to be healthy.

- plenty of **fruit and veg**
  (sample some new ones if you can)

- two or three portions of **protein**
  (such as two small eggs or 100g/4oz tofu*)

- **carbohydrate**
  – a third of your daily diet – and vital for energy

- **dairy foods**
  – rich in calcium for strong bones, teeth and muscles

- **fats and sugars**
  – best not to eat too much of these...

...turn the page to find out why.

*Find out more about ideal portions of protein by visiting **Usborne Quicklinks**.

Good and bad

We need to eat *some* sugar and fat to stay well, but we also need to make sure we eat healthy versions of them whenever we can. Fruit contains natural sugar, and nuts and salmon contain fat – but good, healthy fats. Yes, they really do exist!

When you eat too much food that's crammed with unhealthy sugars (think cakes, cola, biscuits) and unhealthy fats (sausages, cookies, pastry), it's not only bad for your *body*: it can also affect your *mood*, and leave you feeling low. Enjoy these foods when you have them (and we all do), but don't have them too often, basically.

BURP

THE BIG ONE

The absolute baddies

Let's look at one more kind of food that can cause health problems: ultra-processed and/or 'junk food'.

This means food that's been through lots of processes in a factory.

Unfortunately, junk food is, in a way, *clever* food, because it's packed with scrummy things we all crave at times, like LOTS of sugar, salt, fat and **additives**. Media messaging makes it look sooooo tempting, too. But try to enjoy this kind of food only occasionally, because too much of it causes problems such as:

HA! HA!

WEIGHT GAIN

SKIN PROBLEMS

TIREDNESS

FEELING UNFIT & LOSING CONFIDENCE

Hmm, let's not 'go large' today.

97

Learning to eat well

It's time to look at how well YOU eat. Start by making a list of everything you eat for a week, just to see how your diet compares to the 'Eatwell' plate on page 94. If you don't manage to get the balance right, that's fine: it may take time to change your eating habits.

Try eating slowly, mindfully, and enjoying every flavour and mouthful. This is much better for your digestion than wolfing your food down and not really tasting what you're eating. It may help you be less tempted by the not-so-good stuff, too.

Slower is better.

Who knew?

It takes your stomach
20 minutes
to realize it's full.

The choice is yours, always, but try to choose wisely. It's worth it, to help your brain and your body feel as good as they possibly can. Try these healthy tips:

1) For breakfast toast, or lunchtime sandwiches, try to use <u>wholemeal</u> or seeded bread whenever you can.

2) To reach the (5) portions of fruit and veg a day many experts recommend, munch on carrot sticks, apple slices, grapes or a banana as a snack.

3) If you're hungry between meals, try a handful of nuts, microwave popcorn, a fruit smoothie (frozen fruit is fine) or apple slices with peanut butter.
Yum!

4) <u>Think before you eat.</u> This isn't always easy (especially when you're hungry) but your body will only be able to do everything you want it to if you fuel it with good food.

We need water!

OK, so all this information about good food is great, but there's something big missing. A vital ingredient in the 'healthy you' mix is:

staying hydrated

You need to drink enough water to stay hydrated.

If you're finding that:

- it's hard to concentrate,
- you're super snappy, or
- you're getting a lot of headaches,

this could be your body showing you that **you're not drinking enough.** When you realize that up to 60% or our bodies is made up of water, it helps you understand just how important it is.

Opinions vary on how much water we should drink, and if the weather is hot, we need more, of course, but it's a good idea to aim for around 6–8 glasses of water a day. Tap water is usually fine (or filtered, if the tap water is not good where you live) and it's free. Try carrying a refillable bottle to make sure you always drink enough when you're on the go.

Phew! I really need this water.

Me too!

slurp

Dangerous dieting

There is another kind of diet that is focussed on how MUCH you eat rather than WHAT you eat, and it's aimed at helping people lose or gain weight. Sometimes, you need to make some changes to your diet because being overweight or underweight brings its own health issues BUT always worrying about your weight or your size is bad for your physical and your mental health.

Despite the body positivity movement (see page 50) young people can still feel pressured to conform to a certain body shape, and control what they eat. In extreme cases, this can lead to eating-related disorders such as **bulimia** and **anorexia nervosa**.

This is not going to fill me up at ALL.

Basically, your body needs enough good food and will not function well if it doesn't get it, and you could become ill. It sounds simple, but food can be a complex issue for some people. If you feel you or someone you know may have what experts call 'a negative relationship' with food, or perhaps you're worried about a diet that's gone too far, please:

Tell someone you trust
AS SOON AS POSSIBLE

Your GP, your parents or carers, a good friend or your teachers are all good places to start. People will want to help, but you need to reach out and tell them how you feel for them to be able to.

You'll also find lots of sources of help and support at **Usborne Quicklinks**, so you need never feel alone if you're struggling with eating healthily, or with your relationship with food.

Chapter Seven

Taking care of your body

Put simply, bodies are **amazing.**
They fight illness, mend broken bones, grow
new hair and nails, prepare you for being an
adult and enable you to feel and think.

But all this amazingness means that taking care
of your body is *very important*, because a) you
only have one, and b) it needs and deserves it.
This chapter is full of ways of making
sure your body stays healthy without
you running a marathon or eating
a LOT of raw vegetables.

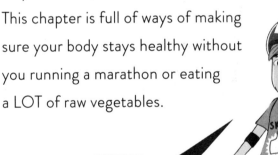

> I need to take
> good care of this
> body of mine.

Get moving

In Chapter 6, you read how important it is to
eat a balanced diet, and think about what you
put *into* your body. Now it's time to think about
what you *do* with your body to keep it working
well. Put simply, you need to

MOVE it!

This means getting some regular, enjoyable,
exercise, starting at a level that works for you.

What does the word 'exercise' actually mean
to you? Something scary, perhaps. Well, in
a dictionary, you'll find it defined very simply:

exercise
an activity involving physical effort
which improves health and fitness

Exercise can take many, many forms, and the one you choose is up to you, but:

You need to DO some to be healthy.

It may surprise you to hear that the recommended amount of exercise for most young people is 60 minutes – yes a whole hour – every day. If this fills you with horror, don't panic: **any** exercise is better than none, and it's fine to start small. In fact, it's better to do that if you haven't been active for a while. The key thing is to **begin**.

There's something else you need to know...

Doing something active isn't only good for your BODY: it's good for your MOOD, too.

Exercise releases chemicals called **endorphins** into the brain, which can make you feel happier.

☑ Healthy

+

☑ Happy = Result!

Let's look at how to build some exercise into your life. If it isn't there already, you are NOT ALONE. There is a big problem with young people not being active enough. One of the main reasons for this is the amount of time spent sitting and looking at screens.

The key is to get the balance right in what you do, and when you do it. Spending some time looking at screens is fine, but too much can be a problem. From time to time, remind yourself that not moving enough, and becoming less healthy, is one problem you are going to avoid. Sorted.

What should I try?

Anything and everything! Whatever gets you moving, gets the blood pumping and your heart beating a little faster is good. Exercise doesn't even have to mean *sport*, but you could try a few and see what you enjoy.

Starting out

When you first start to exercise, it's best to begin with simple, everyday ways of moving your body that you can regularly build into your day. Try:

Walking — start slow and build up the pace over time

Dancing in your bedroom

Skipping in the park

Just go for it!

Moving more

The next stage is
'moderate exercise',
which involves doing
something a little more
vigorous, such as:

Cycling, perhaps
up a gentle hill

Jogging faster, swinging your arms as you go

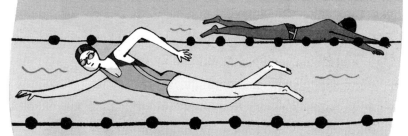

Swimming – at your own pace,
but keep going

Going for it

The next stage, called 'vigorous exercise' is even more energetic, and particularly good for your health and fitness. It's best to build up to this gradually.

It's also very important that you:

I think I can do this. No, I know I can.

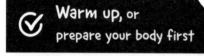

Warm up, or prepare your body first

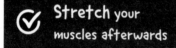

Stretch your muscles afterwards

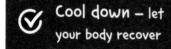

Cool down – let your body recover

These are some warm-up and stretch-out ideas to get you started...

1 Warming up

Before you begin vigorous execise, try swinging your arms in big circles, or lying down and 'cycling' your legs for five minutes.

2 Stretching out

Next, your muscles need to be prepared to work hard. Slowly bend down and try to touch your toes or lift your knees up high at least ten times, to loosen your muscles up.

Now your body is ready for some vigorous exercise, which could include:

- **An aerobics class**
- **Running**
- **Playing rugby**
- **Cycling**

ZIP

3 Cooling down

Afterwards, take time to stretch your muscles gently. Breathe deeply for a few minutes, to help slow your heart rate.

Hopefully, you'll feel

brilliant!

Great workout!

Stick to the plan

It can be all too easy to start off full of good intentions to exercise more, but feel your motivation slip away if other things get in the way (as they often do). If you find this happens to you, don't worry – changing habits is not easy, but don't give up.

Here are a few useful tips to help you:

Motivational Tips

- Have the things you need
(such as a water bottle,
your trainers and a great
playlist) ready to go.

  No more excuses. We're doing this!

- Get a mate on board.
If you both commit to an exercise
routine, you'll encourage each other
(and it's much harder to bottle it).

- Sign up for a regular class, so that
you're committed to go (or risk losing
your money: a great motivator). It can
be yoga, aerobics, cross-fit. Your choice.

- There are lots of great exercise apps
you can download too. Many are free,
and easy to follow. They mean you can
exercise in private, and at your own pace,
if that feels more comfortable for you.

What's best for my body?

Now you know a bit more about exercise, and how important it is, choose one answer to each of these questions.

Q1: It's a lovely, sunny day and one of your mates suggests going on a bike ride. What do you do?

a)   Make an excuse. You're too tired, and it's too hot to do anything really strenuous today.

b)   Get yourself a healthy snack, such as some fruit, fill your water bottle and give it a go!

c)   Say you don't really fancy a bike ride, but are up for a brisk walk around the local park.

Q2: You have always taken the bus to school, but know you could walk if you left a bit earlier. What do you do?

a)   Carry on getting the bus. It's a no-brainer because it means you get another 15 minutes in bed.

b)   Make the decision to walk every day, and set your phone to count your steps to feel extra virtuous.

c)   Commit to walking at least a few times a week, but allow yourself to get the bus if the weather's bad, or you're late.

Q3: You've never enjoyed team sports, but some mates are organizing a fun volleyball game in the park. What do you do?

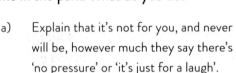

a)   Explain that it's not for you, and never will be, however much they say there's 'no pressure' or 'it's just for a laugh'.

b)   Do it! You've got nothing to lose, and it would be good to spend more time with your mates out in the fresh air.

c)   Tell your friends your reservations, but that you'll come along to the first game and see how you feel.

Q4: One of your friends wants you to go to a new aerobics class with them. You're worried you won't be able to keep up. What do you do?

a)   Tell your mate that you don't enjoy exercising, and would rather relax in other ways than jumping around in a sports hall.

b)   Agree to go along, and give it your best shot. If not now, when? You might really enjoy it!

c)   Say that you'll try one session but may need to take things at your own pace, because you haven't exercised for a while.

Turn the page to see what your answers reveal…

What do my answers mean?

Of course, as with the other quizzes in this book, there is no 'right' answer, but some are much better for your body. If you chose the **a)** answers, that's a shame, because you (and your long-term health) are missing out. If you went for **b)**s, you're super determined to be more active! The **c)** answers are perhaps sensible, 'safe' choices – but how good might you feel if you committed to the **b)** answers?

Chapter Eight

Mental health matters

Your mental health is just as important as your physical health. In fact, the two are so closely linked that if your mental health isn't good, it will probably affect your physical health, and will *definitely* have an impact on your happiness.

It's so tricky to get the balance right.

There's a **lot** of information out there about mental health, which is great, but can be a bit overwhelming. This chapter looks at some of the main mental health problems that affect young people, and offers some tips and tactics for managing them.

Let's look first at what the words 'mental health' actually *mean*. Put simply, it's to do with how we:

Everyone has mental health: it might be 'good', 'OK', or 'not-so-good', but we all have it, all the time, just as we do our physical health.

It's very important for **everyone** to be aware of how good, or not-so-good, they're feeling. Then, it's easier to spot signs that things are not quite right and fix them before they go badly wrong. Mental health issues can be very serious indeed and may need professional help.

Our mental health is linked to our **feelings and emotions** (which are usually a reaction to something, and come and go quite quickly) and our **moods** (that can come from nowhere and can hang around for ages). It probably won't surprise you that young people can find it especially tricky to stay calm and rational when faced with life's challenges, because their moods and feelings are in overdrive, remember? Sadly, this can lead to problems.

SAD news

It's usually easy to tell if you're physically ill: you might feel awful, and have symptoms that you, or a medical professional, can spot. Mental health difficulties can be trickier to identify, because symptoms are less visible and are often thoughts or memories triggered by your brain, (which you also can't see). However, the effect on YOU can be very visible indeed.

Knowing what signs to look for is key and will help you understand, and manage, your feelings – even the negative ones. Here are the three big mental health difficulties that affect a lot of young people:

① STRESS

② ANXIETY

③ DEPRESSION

I think I might need some help.

They can come and go, or stay much longer and really get you down. We'll look at each one closely on the next few pages.

I'm stressed.

That's so stressful.

I don't need this stress.

❶ STRESS

We all experience **stress** at times, but did you know it's actually a *physical* reaction to something your body thinks is a threat, rather than an *emotional* one? Stress releases a chemical called **cortisol** into the body which helped humans deal with imminent danger thousands of years ago, when there were *real* 'life or death' threats to flee from. Today, stress is our body's response to

too much <u>pressure</u>.

For young people, these pressures can come from: school (exams); friendships (needing to fit in); home (parents' or carers' expectations); **social media** (needing to feel more popular/attractive), or a mixture of all these things. Boo.

They may not be threats as grim as a rampaging sabre-toothed tiger, but our bodies perceive them as VERY REAL INDEED.

If you're stressed, your body usually reacts in some, or all, of these ways:

- **Your heart might start racing**
- **Your palms might become a bit sweaty**
- **You might start blinking very quickly**
- **You might 'freeze' and be unable to move**

If you feel like this for a long period of time (because the pressures that are causing your stress are constant) it's a) very damaging to your mental health and b) exhausting.

> You'll find more about how study and school life can cause particular stress, and how to deal with it, in Chapter 9.

❷ ANXIETY

It makes sense that the word **anxiety** comes from the Latin one, *angere*, meaning 'to press or tighten', because, unfortunately, that's how anxiety can make you feel. It's natural to be worried about things at times, such as a test or deadline, but anxiety at a whole new level is a growing problem amongst young people, and it can make even everyday things feel impossible.

There are many kinds of anxiety, but if you experience it in any form, you might have some, or all, of these feelings:

- A deep, constant sense of fear and dread
- You might sweat or shake uncontrollably
- A need to double-check every single thing
- A paralysing feeling of panic

Often, anxiety begins with, or is 'triggered' by, a specific event, but it can also start for no particular reason and then become your default reaction. This can make doing everyday things really difficult at times.

Sadly, because anxiety is invisible, some people find it hard to understand what's happening to you if you're feeling anxious when you're with them. You need to *tell* them.

I'm depressed.

I suffer from depression.

You seem depressed.

❸ DEPRESSION

<u>Depression</u> is a significant mental health difficulty, and is much, much more serious than 'feeling a bit low'. It can affect anyone, even the most happy-go-lucky of people.

It may start after a stressful event, or it can come out of nowhere and descend on your life like a big, black cloud. Signs of depression to look out for in yourself, or a friend, might include:

I can't go on like this.

- Not enjoying things you used to enjoy
- Feeling exhausted all the time
- Not feeling like eating, or seeing anyone
- Thinking you will never be happy again
- Crying a lot, often for no particular reason

Anyone suffering from depression needs care, understanding and patience. They may also need to talk to professionals, and get some medical help, if things don't improve.

Now for the good news

These three mental health problems are increasingly common, but there are ways of helping yourself. If you're worried about how you or someone you know, reacts to problems or difficulties, there are tactics to try. Some might be more helpful than others, and some might take practice, but all are worth a go. Feeling stressed, anxious or depressed – or a nasty combo of all three – is no fun at all. Turn the page for some ways to help you deal with them...

STRESS-BUSTING
TOP TIPS

⭐ **Be aware.** Notice what triggers, say, a panic attack or stomach-clenching anxiety. If you are prepared for a situation, it's easier to manage it by using the tips in this list.

⭐ If you feel yourself experiencing some of the uncomfortable symptoms in this chapter, **break the cycle** by noticing them, pausing, breathing deeply and telling yourself that they will pass. Because they will.

⭐ **Visualize** yourself calm, strong and positive, perhaps in your happy place. The more you do this, the more your brain learns to 'defuse' your distress before it worsens.

⭐ **Focus** very firmly on the here and now. What can you see, hear, smell and touch around you? These things are facts, real things, but the feeling that is worrying you is not.

⭐ If you don't feel things are getting better, **ASK FOR HELP.** Talk to friends, parents or carers, a teacher, your GP, your school counsellor. They need to know, to help you.

Beating the blues

Mental ill health is very serious, but it's important to remember that **everyone** has 'off' days, or feels low, or 'blue', from time to time. It's all part of being that incredibly complex thing called a *human being*. Luckily, there are some pretty simple things you can do that might help you keep a realistic, positive outlook on life, even when it gets tough.

MOVE MORE

In chapter 7, you saw what a positive effect getting moving can have on your mental, as well as your physical, health. If you feel yourself starting to feel anxious, why not dance around the room, do 25 skips with a skipping rope or take a dog (a mate's/neighbour's/anyone's!) for a walk. This might well lift your mood enough to stop it spiralling downwards.

I feel better already.

GET OUTSIDE

Re-connecting with nature can make you feel good. Not getting enough fresh air, or spending time outside, is bad for your mental health. Yup, it's true! Try striding out, and really noticing what's around you – trees, clouds, flowers, buildings, birds. Listen to music or a podcast if you like, but take in your surroundings and let feelgood vibes wash over you. If nothing else, it's better than brooding alone in your room.

TAKE CARE OF YOURSELF

When you feel fed-up, it can be easy to let the basics slide. You might stop eating properly, drink less water, sleep too much or not enough,* not shower or wash your hair. It might not be easy right now, but it's **really important** that you look after yourself in these everyday ways. Not doing so makes things feel worse. And you're worth taking care of, after all.

*See Chapter 10 for lots more about
the importance of the right amount of sleep.

SEE PEOPLE

Make time for people you care about, and who care about you. If you're tempted to dodge meeting up with mates after school because you feel you'll have nothing cheerful to say, think twice. If you think you'd rather eat in your room than join your family, think again. People need people, and even when you least feel like it, connecting with someone else can lift you out of your own gloomy thoughts. If you make time for other people, and think the best of them, they are far more likely to do the same for you.

My mental mindset

The way you look at the world can have a big impact on your mental health and how you get through tricky times. Choose one answer to these questions to find out more about this, an attitude to life that's often called your 'mental mindset'.

Q1: What kind of outlook do you have overall?

a) I usually think things will go wrong, so often miss out on opportunities in case I'm proved right.

b) I'm a cautious person, and a bit anxious, but I'm willing to give most things a go.

c) I never say never. Life's too short to not grab any chance I get to do something fun or new.

Q2: If you've got a problem, what do you tend to do?

a) I keep it to myself. Everyone's got their own worries and they don't want to know about mine.

b) I find one trusted friend to talk to, and ask their advice in confidence.

c) I let my friends and family know what's wrong. That's the only way to sort out problems, isn't it?

Q3: You've noticed that a mate is very anxious at the moment, but you're also busy, and not feeling too good. What do you do?

a)   Give them a wide berth. They will have to get through this tough time, as you're trying to do.

b)   Invite them along to something with other people. You can feel you've tried, and it might make them feel better. That's good enough.

c)   Anxiety is real, as you know. Talk to your mate, and be open and honest. You might find that a problem shared, is a problem solved.

Q4: If you're feeling low, what makes you feel better?

a)   Nothing makes me feel better. I just go over and over the issue in my head until I'm exhausted.

b)   I find listening to music, watching a movie or playing an online game in my bedroom can help.

c)   I try to do something! I might kick a ball in the park, go for a jog or arrange to meet a mate for a chat.

Turn the page to see what your answers reveal...

What do my answers mean?

As you know by now, there's no 'right' answer. We are all different in the way we react to problems and challenges. BUT you can probably see that the **a)** answers reveal a negative mental mindset, the **b)**s a realistic one, and the **c)** answers, a very positive one. Aim to be a balance of **b)** and **c)**, and try to give everything and everyone – including yourself – the benefit of the doubt.

You ARE important

No matter how you feel, you DO matter. You ARE valued. Mental health is a huge and growing area, with countless experts and limitless advice. Sometimes it's not easy to know where best to turn. If you want sound guidance, or more detail on mental health issues, go to **Usborne Quicklinks.**

Remember that if you feel you need help with your mental health, please tell someone immediately.

Help is
out there.

Suicidal thoughts

There's one aspect of mental health that we haven't looked at yet in this chapter, and it's a very serious one. For some people, the only way they can see out of feeling very miserable is to consider ending their life. This is called 'having suicidal thoughts', and particularly affects young men. Thoughts may not become actions, but even *thinking* such things is sad and worrying.

> If, **at any time,** ending your life is something that's even crossed your mind, please, please TALK TO SOMEONE. The people who care about you need to know how you feel, because if they don't, they can't help. And they will want to.

There are also organizations who offer specific guidance and support in this area in a totally non-judgemental way. Again, you'll find them at **Usborne Quicklinks**. Reach out and be honest with the people around you. **You are not alone, and there is ALWAYS a better way than suicide.**

School, and how to survive it

School is a very big part of life for the vast majority of young people. You'll spend a **lot** of time there. (It's probably best not to even *think* about how many hours, days, weeks, months or years. Gulp!)

Ideally, school is where you learn, make friends, start to think about your future and work to make it happen. It's where you feel happy, engaged and part of a big community. Sound good? It can be.

143

But sometimes, school can be stressful:

All these elements are often in the schooldays mix too. Another key factor is that you have no choice about going to school: it's the law. Juggling all these potential sources of stress can be very tricky indeed.

Everyone will have a different experience of school and education, but this chapter aims to help you make the best of yours. It suggests ways of coping with the pressures you, or someone you know, might face at school, because how you *respond* to any of them affects how well you *get through* them. That's something you might not have known...

Resilience

Before we head on into the pressures of school life, it's worth telling you the single most effective defence against all of them. It's called **resilience**, and it's something you can learn, use, and develop, if you practise it enough.

If you look up 'resilience' in a dictionary, you'll find it defined something like this:

resilience
the ability to bounce back or recover quickly from difficulties; toughness

Whatever difficulties you have to face in life (and everyone has to, sometimes) the ability to bounce back from problems and setbacks is an incredibly valuable skill. On the pages ahead, you'll find lots of resilience-building tips to try.

But first, let's look at some of the pressures you might need resilience to cope with...

① Exam pressures

Does *anyone* enjoy exams? They're stressful, they take over your life and you're forever told that so much depends on them. OK, it might,

Save me!

but does that help you cope? Not really. It will probably just make you worried and miserable.

BUT a calm, positive attitude can make a big difference to how you feel and how you cope during stressful times, even exams. The key is to prepare for them as well as you can, remember **that they WILL end and that you WILL survive,** then go into them and *try your best*. That's all you can do, and it's enough.

Here are some tips to help you 'study smart', and stay calm, *before*, *during* and *after* exams:

BEFORE

 You'll be given plenty of warning about exams, so take the opportunity to **prepare yourself:**

- **Eat well**
- **Prioritize sleeping enough**
- **Don't compare your study schedule to others'**

 It's a good idea to **do something active before you sit down to study.** This will get the blood pumping and help you focus. A quick walk, a dance or an active video game all work well.

 Make your study space as uncluttered as possible, with no distractions. If you find you work best listening to music, fine, but turn off **notifications** on any device RIGHT NOW.

It's important to **stay hydrated** (or drink enough water), as this helps you concentrate. Always have water on your desk (so you won't be tempted to go to the kitchen/grab a snack/check your phone).

 Decide how long you are going to study for. Research shows that the brain learns best for shorter periods of time, rather than long stretches.

 Work out a 'study schedule' and try to stick to it. Blocks of one to two hours work best with a five-minute break every half hour, or a ten-minute break every hour.

DURING

 Try to **get enough sleep** the night before each exam and **eat healthy, energy-giving food.**[*] A late-night revision session, sugary comfort food, energy drinks and a takeaway pizza are not ideal brain fodder!

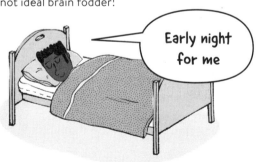

*Find ideas for healthy snacks at **Usborne Quicklinks**.

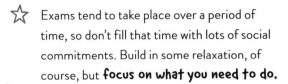 Exams tend to take place over a period of time, so don't fill that time with lots of social commitments. Build in some relaxation, of course, but **focus on what you need to do.**

☆ **Don't rush.** Settle yourself down and take some deep breaths. When you turn over your paper, read it slowly and carefully, perhaps a couple of times, as the words may not sink in at first.

☆ If, at any time, you begin to feel a bit panicky, **try not to let worry get a grip on you.** Pause, sit back, let your shoulders relax and close your eyes for a few deep breaths. You've got this.

☆ If you're flagging, **spur yourself on by visualizing your happy place,** or see yourself sitting down for some food you really love later today. Life really will go on, whatever happens in this exam. Honestly.

So, **it's over!** You might feel ecstatically confident, or you might not. However you feel, you survived it and hopefully, you feel you did your best. Be proud of what you've achieved.

AFTER

☆ If there are more exams ahead, make sure you **build in some kind of break after each one.** Get yourself moving, get outside, do things you enjoy and then, go again.

☆ **Try not to brood about your answers.** This isn't easy, especially if your mates all seem to be telling you they've nailed it, but a 'postmortem' probably won't help, and could get you down.

☆ **Look forward, not back.** If this exam didn't go as well as you'd hoped, try to see yourself as someone with lots more chances ahead, and who's still learning, and still trying.

☆ **Reflect.** How was the experience for you? Was it as stressful as you feared, or actually not that bad? Could you have coped better? If so, **think about how to improve, for next time.**

❷ Friendship pressures

The friends you make in school are key to your happiness. Chapter 5 looked at how to choose, and how to be, a good friend, but it's helpful to have some 'resilience' tips for when relationships in school become stressful. This can happen for many different reasons, but here are some of the main ones:

Being left out

You may sometimes feel on the edge of a group of friends, or left out. This is tough, but **it's not your fault that others can be unkind.** Wait, without losing your cool or doubting yourself: hopefully, it will pass.

FOMO

The 'fear of missing out', aka '**FOMO**', is a very real pressure. It can lead you to make unwise decisions for fear of losing out on an experience or an opportunity. Aim to stop, and **think about whether it's worth it before you decide what to do (or not do).**

Peer pressure

Other young people (your **peers**) may urge you to do things you aren't happy doing. It's not easy, but try to **stick to your values, and do what you feel is best.** You're the one that matters, after all.

Come on, EVERYONE's doing it...

Bullying

This is a very serious problem indeed. Nobody has the right to bully you, and nobody deserves to be bullied. Don't suffer in silence. **Tell someone you trust, and ask for help.*** (It's often much easier to have tricky conversations like this when you're not facing the other person, by the way.)

*There's advice and details of organizations that can help you manage bullying at **Usborne Quicklinks**.

③ Parent/carer pressures

Your parents or carers want the very best for you, but they can, unwittingly, put pressure on you when it comes to schoolwork and exams. To them, they are encouraging you to achieve your full potential, but to you, it can feel like nagging, and you probably worry about disappointing them. Sound familiar?

The best way of resolving this kind of pressure is to TALK TO EACH OTHER. The adults in your life can't know what's going on inside your head unless you tell them. Perhaps, together, you can come up with a way of managing school commitments that doesn't feel as overwhelming, or one-sided. If you listen to and respect each other's viewpoint, you're halfway there.

Dad, can we talk?

Pressure points

So, do you feel a bit better prepared to tackle the pressures of school life now? Choose one answer to these questions to find out:

Q1: Exams are starting soon, but some of your mates are going to a festival in the middle of them. What do you do?

a)   Go the festival. You wouldn't want to miss out on that much fun and your friends won't forgive you if you don't go with them.

b)   Look at your schedule. Would you still be ready for the exams before and after the festival, if you went? Would it really be worth the risk?

c)   Decide to give it a miss this time. There will be plenty more festivals and you need to give the exams your best shot, for your own wellbeing. You owe yourself that.

WOOOOO!

YEAH!

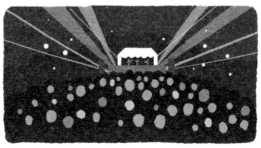

Q2: Your friendship group has started meeting every lunchtime on the playing field, but they haven't invited you along. What do you do?

a) Stay out of their way. If they haven't invited you, they can't want to be friends with you any more. That's just the way it is.

b) Go along and join them anyway. Perhaps they just forgot to tell you, and it's better to know the truth than to guess at it...

c) Tell them that you're hurt, and feel that you want to find other, kinder people to hang out with if they're going to behave like that.

Q3: All your family talks about is how important it is that you do well at school. You're trying your hardest, but it's getting you down. What do you do?

a) Say nothing and hope the conversations about school are short ones. If you argue, it will only make things worse.

b) Leave the room if and when this subject is raised yet again. At least you won't have to listen any more.

c) Talk to your family about how you feel. Explain that you're doing your best, but you're feeling pressured by their attitude.

Turn the page to see what your answers reveal...

What do my answers mean?

If you went for the **a)** answers in
this quiz, perhaps you need to value
yourself a little more and face up to
challenges a bit better. If you chose
the **b)** answers, they are reasonable
compromises, but do you think you'd
feel happy in the longer term if you
did what they suggest? Probably not.
The **c)** answers show real self-respect
and resilience, so if you chose them,
well done! You matter (in school or
anywhere else) and those around you
need to know it.

Sleep, and how to get enough of it

Sleep is as essential to our health as food and water. Without enough rest, you will probably be a) tired, b) grumpy, c) tearful and moody, d) have sore eyes and heavy-feeling limbs. If this goes on for a while, you can probably add e) being unable to concentrate, f) feeling physically unwell and g) being pretty miserable into the mix. Sound grim? Well, it can be.

I'm soooo tired. I need some sleep right now.

Sleep is much more than just some hours spent lying on a bed at night-time. It's the time when our bodies recharge, our brains reboot and our memories, worries and thoughts are processed, and often 'filed away'. Everyone needs to sleep enough to live a fit, full and fulfilled life.

For many people, getting the right amount of sleep can be a problem, however. This has a knock-on effect on their mood, and their ability to do all the many things they need to do in a day. Let's find out why...

The sleep cycle

During every night, your body goes through separate stages of sleep, lots and lots of times. The most restorative, beneficial stage is called **REM sleep** (which stands for **R**apid **E**ye **M**ovement). If you're woken up during this fifth and final stage, the deepest part of your sleep cycle, you're probably going to feel *rough*.

1 DROWSY
First 5–10 mins

2 LIGHT SLEEP
10–25 mins

3 MODERATE SLEEP
20–40 mins

4 DEEP SLEEP
30 mins

5 REM SLEEP
20–40 mins

The Sleep Cycle

Unfortunately for young people, it's not easy for them to 'tune into' this cycle, because they often go to sleep so late. Why? Because their bodies don't release the sleep-triggering hormone **melatonin** until later in the evening than adults' bodies do. Which then means that they don't want to go to sleep until later at night (and so *certainly* don't want to wake up for school).

Research shows that, ideally, young people need:

8 to 10 hours of sleep
EVERY night

(which means that they need to be in bed at around 10.30pm to be rested and up for school at around 7.30am the next morning). An increasing number of young people are not getting *anywhere near* that amount. Not great.

Many are awake until the early hours (often looking at electronic devices, ahem!). They are then exhausted the following day, hoping that **adrenaline** (a chemical the body releases when it's stressed or excited) will get them through. Some turn to sugary food or energy drinks as a quick fix, but these are neither a solution, nor healthy: in fact, they're the opposite, and can make you feel *worse*.

Naps are a good idea, if no longer than 20 minutes and not too late in the day, but napping on your desk in double maths isn't really an option, is it?

Tough news

It's tempting to lie in late at the weekends, because you're shattered, but unfortunately you can't 'bank' sleep, and long lie-ins can affect your sleep for the *next* night, or even longer. Sorry to break this to you, folks.

Not getting enough sleep is not good for you at all, basically. Every day is tough, and it's easy to feel you can't get a grip on schoolwork, feel good or enjoy your life. But despite the way your teenage brain is wired, all is not lost sleep-wise, and you *can* change things for the better. Read on.

Sleep top tips

Improving your sleep pattern will take time and effort, because there is no one-size-fits-all solution, but it can be done. If you consistently embed these tips into your bedtime routine, you'll notice things slowly getting better. So what can you do to sleep better?

- **DO get some exercise and fresh air at some point every day.**
- **DO try a warm bath or shower, then pop on your cosiest pjs.**

But maybe not just before bed!

- **DO read a book or listen to a podcast.**
- **DO listen to some slow, soothing music, or a relaxing soundtrack.**
- **DO have a small snack, such as toast, a banana or a bowl of cereal.**
- **DO have a warm milky drink.**
- **DO make your room a cool, calm, darkened space.**

Think about blackout curtains or blinds, and leave your window open a crack.

What to avoid

Equally, there are 'top tips' for what NOT to do when it comes to sleep. Keep these in mind and avoid them if you want a good night's sleep:

- **DON'T look at any screen for an hour before you need to sleep.**
- **DON'T keep your phone in the room you sleep in.**
- **DON'T drink energy drinks, or caffeinated drinks after lunch.**
- **DON'T eat lots of heavy, filling food late at night.**
- **DON'T take long naps, especially after school in the early evening.**
- **DON'T do a late night workout.**

If you find that too tricky, turn it off, or put it on silent.

There are lots more tips to help you relax and sleep well at **Usborne Quicklinks**. Experts call them 'sleep hygiene'.

Mind and body

Your body's ready for sleep, but what about your *mind*? If you find your brain is buzzing when you want to fall asleep, try some of these techniques for getting yourself into the zone:

✔ **Get everything ready for the next day.** Lay your clothes out and pack your bag with all you'll need.

✔ **If things are worrying you, write them down.** You can deal with them tomorrow.

✔ **Close your eyes and slow your breathing right down.** Breathe in and out, following a steady rhythm for several minutes if you can.

✔ **Feel each part of your body begin to relax** – your toes, your legs, your tummy, your chest, all the way up to your face and the top of your head.

✔ **Don't panic if you just can't relax.** Keep breathing slowly and deeply, focusing on each breath. Your body and mind are still resting. It's all good.

Keep a notebook next to your bed for these niggles.

If you practise, you'll find that these things become a calming routine that your brain recognizes as a prompt to relax, and sleep.

The 'sleep well' quiz

Now that you know how important sleep is, and the problems that can arise if you don't get enough of it, choose one answer to each of these questions:

Q1: You're struggling to stay awake in afternoon lessons. Your mate offers you an energy drink. What do you do?

a) Down the lot. It will give you a bit of a lift for a while, and you'll just have to cope with the 'slump' afterwards.

b) Splash your face with cold water, have a good, long drink of water and decide to get to bed earlier that evening.

c) Only drink some of the energy drink. Hopefully, that sugar hit will be enough get you through.

Q2: You and a friend are at the final level of a game, but it's 11pm on a Tuesday. What do you do?

a) Keep going until you finish it. It's much more important than sleep.

b) Tell your mate you need to sleep now, or you'll feel rubbish tomorrow.

c) You need to be up at 7am, but surely one more hour won't hurt.

We're finally here!

Q3: There's a lot going on for you at the moment, and you're finding it really difficult to get to sleep. What do you do?

a) Chat to your friends about what's worrying you. They're always out there, even at night and you need their support now.

b) Write your worries down, then put them out of your mind. You can't solve problems now: you're tired. Maybe tomorrow...

c) Choose just one of your worries, and focus on trying to think of a solution to it. That will be one off your list, anyway.

Q4: Your room is a complete mess; you hate being in it, and are finding it difficult to sleep in there too. What do you do?

a) I eave it. There's more to life than a super tidy bedroom. You'll crash when you're tired enough.

b) Sort it out. Set aside a time to do it, and give it a thorough clean and tidy. Now keep it like that.

c) Change your bedding. Having nice, fresh bedding might make a bit of a difference. The rest can wait.

What do my answers mean?

You'll be aware by now that there are no 'right' answers, but some show a much healthier attitude to sleep, and taking care of yourself, than others. If you chose **a)**s, you're not giving your body the opportunity to rest enough. The **c)**s are a compromise, but the **b)** answers prioritize sleep. You need to try to do that to feel alert and well-rested.

Sleep really does matter – try to get enough of it.

Chapter Eleven

Social media – good, bad or both?

Can you *imagine* life without social media?
No phones, no notifications, no photos, no likes,
no alerts, no apps, no chats? OK, be honest:
does that sound like a good thing, a totally bad
thing, or something in between? And what do
you think your parents' or carers' answers would
be? They may be able to remember life before
social media (and if so, will probably have told
you how much simpler/quieter/
better things were then
many, many times. Zzzz).
Yup, social media can
divide the crowds.

I could really do with some social media in my life right now.

173

But what, actually, *is* this thing we call social media? Well, put very simply, it means interacting with other people online rather than in person, face-to-face. There are lots of different ways of doing this, but the key characteristic of all of them is that they're online, and this is where problems can lie.

For the majority of young people, all around the world, social media is a *huge and important* part of modern life. It connects you to people, to the outside world and to endless information, which is great, but there are some very real downsides. Let's take a closer look.

Good... and not so good

This chapter looks at both sides of social media.

Let's start with some of the positives...

Social media can:

- Help you **stay in touch with people,** especially those you don't see very often.

- **Tell you what you want to know quickly** (if not always reliably. Always check the facts.)

- Help you **let several people know about something** quickly and easily and **organize stuff.**

- **Keep you up to date** on worldwide news, alerts for gig tickets, local events and lots more.

- Help you **find people you have things in common with,** such as fan groups or fellow gamers.

- Make it **easier to start getting to know someone** if you feel shy about face-to-face meet-ups.

It's clear that social media can be a really good thing, BUT (you knew that was coming, didn't you?) there are some negatives, too. It can also:

- **Gobble up a LOT of your time,** scrolling through trivia or messaging mates for hours.

- Encourage you to **compare yourself to others,** perhaps not in a positive, healthy way.

- Tempt you into **buying things you don't need** (and often can't afford).

- **Show you things you didn't want or mean to see,** but can't forget once you have.

- **Expose you to unkind things** that people wouldn't say in person because they can be anonymous online.

- **Lead to addiction.** Yes, you can get so hooked on reading, responding, scrolling and liking that you find it hard to stop.

Get off your phone!

I can't! I might miss something!

Now, let's zoom in on how social media adds, or takes away, from you being happy in yourself.

The 'happy' stuff:

- 'Likes' make you feel good. When you get them, your body releases a tiny shot of those feel-good endorphins that you also get when you exercise.
- Chilling by playing a game or chatting with someone on social media can be a welcome relief from the pressures of school and teenage life.
- Connecting with people online can help you manage or solve problems by discussing them.

  Especially if you can't easily do this face-to-face.

- Discovering music, movies, books, blogs and podcasts that you enjoy is a massive plus in your life, and will bring you a lot of happiness. Hurrah!

All good... and social media can also influence your health in several positive ways:

The 'healthy' stuff:

- Finding out about things you can do, learn, or get involved in, is a great thing to do.

But remember to DO those things, not just read about them.

- Sharing thoughts and ideas with others can be good for your mental health: social connection is important for everyone. Just make sure you're kind, always.

- Doing a regular yoga class, exercise session, or dance routine online is not as sociable as going to a 'real' one, but it's MUCH better than not doing them at all.

- Making positive changes to your lifestyle is easy if you research carefully online for, say, healthier food options or a do-able exercise plan. There's no judgement, no shaming and lots of hope and possibility.

Great stuff

Hopefully, this chapter has shown you that social media can be a really good thing. It can help you form and strengthen connections with people you might never meet in person; it offers you a world of information and entertainment and can make you feel part of a supportive and inclusive community if you use it with care. All these things are good.

Great to talk to you both!

We have so much in common.

I feel like I've made two new friends.

BUT...

Forming lasting, meaningful relationships with other people is vital to our happiness as human beings: **people need people.**

Social media is great in very many ways, but it's no substitute for face-to-face contact with a real-life person.

HA! HA!

Bring in the balance

The message to take away from this chapter is a simple one:

Don't let your online life become so important that you don't live your 'real' one.

This can happen more easily than you might think: often, it's a gradual, creeping process, until it becomes something you can't control.

At the extreme end of this **addiction** to social media are young people who are online 24/7, and live as recluses who never go out, which is so sad because they are missing out on life. In Japan, they are called '**hikikomori**'.

Try to use social media safely and sensibly to *enrich* your life: dip into things, read about issues that interest you and join groups that make you feel welcome, but always stay rooted in the real world, with real people. Remember that, all too often, the 'facts' posted online are not actually true, and the images don't represent how life actually is. They are edited, filtered and curated to present a happier, glossier version. When it comes to social media, a balanced approach is best, always.

THE WORLD NEEDS HUGS
Real ones.

How much does it matter to me?

If you recognized some of the pros and cons of social media in this chapter, that's a sound start. Now it's time to see how big a role it plays in your life by choosing one answer to each of these questions:

Q1: Your friends are all posting new, uber-filtered profile pics. What do you do?

a)   The same thing, of course! Filters always make you feel so much happier about how you look in photos.

b)   Don't bother updating your pic. It's not important, and those filters can make you look weird, anyway.

c)   See if you can find a pic you like, so that you can post a new one, but go for 'fun' filters if you use any at all.

Q2: Someone has posted a nasty comment about you online, but kept their identity hidden. What do you do?

a) Have an absolute meltdown, and frantically ask all your friends if they know who posted it. Then post an equally nasty reply.

b) Delete it. It happens, and it's hurtful, but it's not worth your time or energy even thinking about it.

c) Feel upset, and ask a few friends if they know anything. Then put down your phone for a while and do something positive, that you enjoy.

Q3: You've got spots, and you've seen an ad on social media for a cream that promises miracles, but it's very expensive. What do you do?

a) Get it. Beg your parents or carers to lend you the money if you have to. Those 'before and after' photos can't lie, can they?

b) Dismiss it. It's just one more expensive con to get you to part with money you haven't got for something that probably doesn't work.

c) Check out the reviews, and see if you can find out more about the product and its results. Then decide whether to commit the cash.

Turn the page to see what your answers reveal...

What do my answers mean?

As you've probably guessed, if you chose the **a)** answers, social media is REALLY important in your life. You use it, trust it and need it. If you went for the **b)**s, you can take it or leave it, as it isn't a key part of your life. If you chose the **c)**s, you have a sensible, balanced attitude to social media. You can see its advantages, but don't let it rule your life. Go you!

It's all about the money

Everyone needs money, to pay for food, clothes and somewhere safe to live. Luckily, your parents or carers will usually cover these basic needs for you, but money will still have a big role to play in your life. You may have an allowance, a part-time job to pay for treats, want to make the most of some savings, or *always* feel broke. Whichever one is you, money matters, to everyone.

I'm a part-time dog walker to earn some cash.

Money is no guarantee of happiness, though: far from it, in fact. But not having *enough* money can make you very *unhappy*, which can then impact on your wellbeing in many different ways. Perhaps your family, or people you know, sometimes struggle financially? If so, you'll know this can be very difficult indeed.

Luckily, as a young person, the money you have will be mainly for 'extras' rather than 'essentials', but learning how to *manage* your money, however much of it you have, can make life a whole lot easier. Knowing the value of money is a skill that will always stand you in good stead, so we really need a chapter about it in this book!

299.99

Ouch! Is that what they always cost?

Hidden dangers

Every day, we're bombarded with ads, offers, messages, buy-now-pay-later sites and push notifications, all aimed at getting us to part with our cash (whether we actually have it, or not) so that other people can get more money. Some experts call this the 'buy/get/have' culture. Hmmm... doesn't sound very appealing, does it?

Having new stuff is great, and gives you a buzz of those feel-good endorphins, but buying things can also lead to problems that last a lot longer than that buzz. Turn the page to find out some things to consider.*

*Remember, you'll find lots more info about being money-savvy at **Usborne Quicklinks**.

1 'Need' or 'want'?

Before you press 'buy it now', ask yourself this simple question:

Do I <u>need</u> it or do I just <u>want</u> it?

Here's the difference between the two:

NEEDS are necessities, like new shoes when yours are too small or worn out.

WANTS are impulses or desires for something that, if you're honest, you'd actually be fine without.

OMG! I really want that dress!

Dress to Impress

② Buy now, but can't pay later?

One aspect of the 'buy/get/have' culture is proving a particular problem for young people, because they often make very impulsive decisions. This means that the buy-now-pay-later option that many websites offer really appeals to them. The *consequences* come later, but it seems do-able at the time.

So I need to pay for this in 30 days. No problem!

If you're tempted, remember to think about **how you are actually going to pay** when the payment is due. If you don't *know* how, don't commit to buying. The same applies to the 'pay in 3 instalments' sometimes offered. Sure, the first instalment may be manageable, but the other two will also need paying pretty soon... Gulp!

3 Loans and borrowing

If you have your own bank account, you can organize any regular payments you need to make, such as subscriptions for streaming platforms, get alerts when you're running low on cash and see how much you're spending, and on what. You won't be able to get a loan from most banks until you're at least 18, but don't be tempted to borrow money from friends or family unless you're sure you can repay it in a way that suits you both. Not doing so will make you feel bad, and probably ruin your relationship. It's just not worth it.

LOCK

Know your limits

Basically, when it comes to cash, it's a good idea to know how much you have, or are expecting to have, before you make any plans to spend it. This is called **budgeting** (which basically means staying in control of your money). You could set up a simple spreadsheet on your phone or computer,* or have a notebook to jot down your spending in. Here are the steps to follow:

Step 1

Make a note of how much money you get each week. This is called your **income**, and might include an allowance, or wages from a part-time job such as babysitting.

I love kids, so I do some babysitting for our neighbours.

Oooo, ba-ba

*There's a budget spreadsheet to download at **Usborne Quicklinks**.

Step 2

List the things you have to pay for, no choice about it. These are your **expenses** and may include bus fares or lunches at school.

- school snacks
- bus to volleyball
- subs for coach
- pay Joel back
- bubble tea

Step 3

Now, take your expenses away from your income. The amount you have left over is how much money you have left to spend on non-essential things.

Step 4

If you make sure your expenses are never more than your income, you might not have to say 'no' to that cinema trip. **You'll be managing your money.**

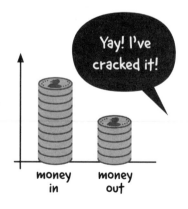

Yes, it can be really tricky to resist all those temptations to spend, but try to remember that, if you go rogue and blow your budget, you may well regret it later. It's worth getting into the habit of *thinking twice before you splurge*. Young people can get into financial trouble very easily and that's no fun at all. These simple questions and tips can help you stay on track:

CLOTHES

- Is it worth it?
- How often will you wear it?
- Will you still like it next week?
- Will it go with your other clothes?

ONLINE

- Save it, and think about it.
- Remember to include the delivery cost.
- Can you return it if you need to?
- Have you read any reviews?

FOOD

- Take a packed lunch instead of buying food.
- Don't shop when you're hungry.
- Don't go near the snacks aisle.
- Do you really need extra fries?

Hmmm

"Being happy costs money!"

It's easy to believe that statement, isn't it?
That's the messaging that surrounds us...

But research shows that the things that
make us the happiest are rarely the ones
that we buy. The real happiness-makers
are experiences, doing stuff we enjoy and
spending time with our friends (and even
our families!). Unexpected, but true...

Here are some ideas for having some fun with the people you like without splashing too much cash:

Have a karaoke session, and just go for it. How about the 'worst' singer wins?

Club together to buy ingredients and do some cookie-baking.

Yesss!

Hold a 'promises challenge', in which each of you has to commit to doing something unusual.

I promise to wear black lipstick all day.

I promise not to speak at all on Saturday.

Give each other a make-over. If you can afford wash-out hair colour, do that too!

Hold a pre-loved/upcycled clothes swap fashion show.

I adore this dress!

I really love this jacket.

Have a 'biggest bargain' contest. Check out those special offers for the absolute cheapest thing (but don't actually buy it!).

70% OFF

Good money habits

So, now you know that you don't need lots of money to be happy, and that it's no guarantee of happiness if you have it. There are lots of miserable millionaires out there!

It seems that happiness actually lies in the middle ground, when you have enough money not to have to worry, and to be able to treat yourself from time to time. There will **always** be more things to see/want/buy, but if you **stop and think first,** you'll have a) a healthy approach to money, and b) probably more of it in your account/purse/wallet!

Right now, I don't need a single thing.

Spender, saver or both?

It's time to find out how good, or not-so-good, you are at managing your money. Choose one answer to these questions – and be honest!

Q1: You've got your eye on a pair of trainers that cost all your month's allowance. What do you do?

a) Get them. You'll worry about how to get through the month with zero cash later.

b) Decide whether you can get through a whole month without buying anything else. Then stick to your decision.

c) Forget it. They're just not worth going without all the other things you might need.

Q2: All your mates are going out for pizza on Friday, but you really can't afford it this month. What do you do?

a) Go! You can't be the only one who doesn't. Ask your mum for a loan (and hope she forgets about it because she's so busy).

b) Offer to do some jobs to raise the cash, or go along and just order a drink. Nobody will mind.

c) Tell your mates you can't make it, and why. If they care about you, they'll understand. There's always next time...

Q3: You really want to join a new weekly drama class in town, but it's quite expensive. What do you do?

a)   Tell your parents/carers that everyone else is going and how much you will get out of it. Surely they can't refuse to pay then?

b)   Go along for the first class. Then, if you think it's worth it, see if you can do some chores to earn enough cash to go each week.

c)   Give it a miss. If you commit to paying for that class every week, you'll have hardly anything left over for other stuff.

Q4: One of your mates comes from a wealthy family, and always suggests expensive outings. What do you do?

a)   Say nothing, and just go along with it! Life's short, and something will come up when you need cash, surely?

b)   Go once in a while, but suggest less expensive things to do as well. Perhaps they'll get the hint!

c)   Ask the others in your group if this makes them uncomfortable, too. If it does, kindly tell your rich mate and explain how you all feel.

Shall we go on a hike this weekend?

Turn the page to see what your answers reveal...

What do my answers mean?

If you went for the **a)** answers, you
have a fairly irresponsible attitude
to money, which could get you into
trouble! If you chose **b)**s, well done:
you know the value of money and
make spending decisions carefully.
The **c)** answers show admirable
self-control, but perhaps you could
allow yourself a little bit of spending
now and then. Life is out there ;-)

Chapter Thirteen

Relationships, and how to survive them

The word 'relationship', put simply, means 'a connection with someone else', and it can take many, many forms. You'll have LOTS of *different* kinds of relationship in your life – with friends, family, classmates, teachers, coaches and even with your pets (if you have any). Relationships are the 'glue' that bonds us to others, and make life richer... but they can be complicated, too.

I'm so happy to be part of this brilliant team!

As a teen, you're developing and changing all the time, both physically and emotionally. You may start to have, or to want to have, a close, loving relationship with someone else. This is a time of learning, experimenting and self-discovery – all good – but do you remember those hormones that are racing around your body? Well, they can make it a bit tricky to make sound choices in the relationships you form. In fact, you may feel you need some guidance through what can feel new, confusing, exciting and even a little scary. If this is you, this chapter's here to help.

Another message from Amy. Do I reply? What should I say?

How will my body change?

Your body will change in many ways during your teenage years, as it's going through a process called **puberty**. These changes are triggered by special 'sex hormones' that your brain tells your body to release when the time is right. Then, it's all systems go, your body takes over and the end result of these gradual changes is the adult you. Ta-da! How amazing is that?

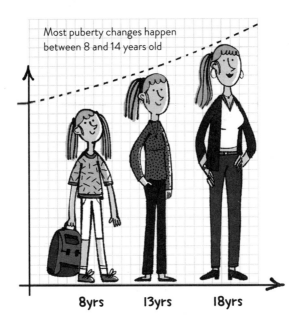

Most puberty changes happen between 8 and 14 years old

8yrs   13yrs   18yrs

What to look for

Here are the main physical changes of puberty, but they happen at different times for different people, and vary for boys and girls. Don't worry about being left behind. Your time will come.

Among other things, young women will find:

- **Their breasts getting bigger and more tender.**
- **Hair growing between their legs and under their arms.**
- **That they start having their monthly periods (called 'menstruation').**

Well, that's new...

Young men will find:

- **Their voice getting lower, or 'breaking' (though it may get squeaky first).**
- **Their penis getting larger and their testicles (balls) dropping lower down.**
- **Hair growing on their face and bodies (especially under their arms and around their genitals).**

Oh no! What was THAT noise?!

SQUEAK

Most young people going through puberty will probably have oilier skin and greasier hair, and perhaps some spots. These things will pass, but they can be a bit of a pain.*

*You'll find tips for managing spots at **Usborne Quicklinks**.

Relationship checklist

When you find yourself physically attracted to other people, your feelings will change, too. This is often called 'fancying' someone, and it's usually a combination of a whole lot of emotions and sensations. You might feel breathless when you see them, blush, be lost for words or feel your heart beating a bit faster, for instance. It's exciting, but scary.

Feeling this way about someone – be it someone of the opposite sex or the same sex as you – marks the start of an exciting new stage of growing up, but it's also unknown territory. Try to keep some basic 'relationship ground rules' like these in mind as you dip your toe into these (wonderful but choppy) waters:

 Remember...

KINDNESS
Everyone deserves kindness, always.
Treat others as you hope they will treat you.

RESPECT
Every single one of us is different. Respect others and expect them to respect you.

ACCEPTANCE
You don't have the right to judge others for the decisions or choices they make. They are them, and you are you.

BE TRUE TO YOURSELF
If something feels wrong in a relationship, or you don't feel valued, trust yourself. You can end it at any time. Honestly.

OK, so these are sound principles, but things are rarely that simple, are they? It's inevitable that some relationships will work out, some won't and some will probably hurt you quite a lot. Luckily, this is how you find out how relationships work, but it can be a steep learning curve. You'll find out what you need and what you want from a partner in time, but there may be a few bumps in the road until you do. That's life, really.

Hidden influences

Whoever you choose to have a relationship with, there may be influences at play that you aren't even aware of. Among the most powerful is holding an opinion about someone based on a set idea of how their **gender** (male or female) should be, and behave. Let's take a closer look at this:

Stereotypes

What dreams do you have for the future? Do you have a career in mind yet, or fancy doing some travelling first? If you're a young woman, you're in luck in many parts of the world. But, in the past, your options would probably have been limited to:

1. Getting married and having kids – perhaps lots of kids.

2. Not getting married and being seen as a sad and lonely 'spinster'.

3. Being quiet, modest and agreeing with mens' opinions.

...and if you're a young man, your options would probably have been:

1. Working hard for most of your life, often for poor pay.

2. Having to support your family single-handedly.

3. Being tough, macho and emotionally stifled.

These are stereotypes, of course, but they were beliefs people held for many years. Although things have improved HUGELY,* traces of these attitudes still remain.

Make it your mission to be aware of them and to question them, every time.

*though not everywhere in the world, sadly.

For instance, if you're a young man, you might hear people:

- Saying **disrespectful**, sexist things to girls or women.
- **Dismissing** the opinions and rights of girls and women.
- Urging young men to be **aggressive** and unkind to women.

Or you might see or hear people:

- **Assuming** that women can't do things that of course they can.
- **Shaming** women by commenting on their body or appearance.
- **Ignoring women's boundaries** and their right to personal space.

NOBODY deserves to be talked about or treated in this way.

This behaviour has a name: **toxic masculinity**. The clue's in the name. It's poisonous, so don't be a part of it. Aim for *healthy* masculinity, which means a fair and non-judgemental approach to everyone. Stereotyping can affect young men, too. You might hear people:

- **Tell other men to 'man up', and not express their emotions freely.**
- **Expect men to dress, speak and behave in a certain, 'macho' way.**
- **Encourage men to brag about their sexual experiences.**

If you're a young woman, do **you** ever expect a young man to stick to this stereotype in any way? It's easily done, but now you know...

Be aware of stealthy stereotyping. It's not good at all.

Mine, not yours

Your body is your own, and only you have the right to decide *what* happens to it and *when* it happens. This is called giving your **consent**. If you don't give that consent, **NOBODY has the right to do anything to your body that you don't want them to do.** What's called 'the age of consent' (when you can legally have sex) around the world varies from around 14 to 18 years old, but the decision is ALWAYS yours, every single time.

Wait. STOP! I don't feel comfortable.

CONSENT IS YOURS TO GIVE, OR REFUSE.

NO MEANS NO!

There is a lot of recent research into mens' attitudes to girls, women and their bodies. It shows that some influencers, and an increase in young people watching **porn**, have fuelled a deeply unhealthy attitude to women and to sex. People in porn films may often look like they are having fun, but many of them – especially young women – are being exploited. They have been forced into doing it, often because they desperately need the money. Porn is not an expression of closeness and love, as sex can be, and it's **not** what you should aim for in a relationship. Set your sights on more positive, healthier, attitudes and behaviours.

Free to be me

Your generation has more freedom to explore your **sexuality** (who you feel attracted to) and your **gender identity** (who you feel yourself to be, male, female, gender fluid or non-binary) than at any other time in history. Again, this is sadly not the case everywhere.

As a young person, you may not be sure who your real 'self' is yet, but that's fine: it's a process, and there's no hurry.

Don't feel pressured into making choices or decisions you're unsure about. You are still developing, and your sexuality may change and develop too. It can be a confusing area, with lots of ideas, opinions and emotions at play.

As you navigate your way through puberty, it helps to be surrounded by supportive, understanding people. If this is not how it is for you, there are places you can go for help and advice, but you need to be able to talk about how you feel with someone. Not doing so can potentially lead to unhappiness and, all too often, mental health problems.

Hopefully, you'll find those that care about you more responsive than you think, and willing to be open about *their* worries, too. This is the two-way connection at the heart of any healthy relationship. Remember, above all: **you are important, and you have a right to be you – whoever that 'you' may be.**

You'll find lots more information, and suggestions for where to ask for advice on many aspects of relationships, sexuality and gender at **Usborne Quicklinks**.

Relationship goals

This chapter has looked at some pretty serious stuff, but it's *important* stuff, that needs to be discussed. It's vital that you make kind, respectful decisions in *every* relationship you have in your life. That's how we'll build a happier you and a healthier society.

What's the best choice?

Can you answer these relationship-based questions?

 Q1: One of your mates is in a relationship, but all they tell you is how unhappy and unappreciated they feel. What do you do?

a) Tell them to stop telling you about it if they're not going to end it. It's pointless and it's boring.

b) Listen, say nothing and let them tell you all the details (again). One day it might be you, needing them to listen.

c) Tell them that you sympathize, but feel it's time they took some positive action. They deserve better than this.

Q2: You think about your sexuality a lot, and are having a lot of confusing feelings. What do you do?

a) Say nothing, and do nothing. It will be a whole lot easier if you just keep your feelings to yourself. They may pass.

b) Do some research and find out where you could get more information and advice before you talk to anyone about it.

c) Talk to your parents or carers and friends openly and honestly.

Q3: Someone in your friendship group keeps upsetting the girls in your school by commenting on their appearance in an unkind way. What do you do?

a) Nothing! It's only banter, and the girls know it. Everyone says stuff like that, don't they? No real harm done.

b) Explain to the girls that you really don't agree with this kind of behaviour. That's better than nothing, surely?

c) Call it out. Nobody has the right to belittle, judge or insult anyone else. Those days are gone – or should be. Tell your mate to cut it out.

Q4: You're in a relationship, and really like your partner, but they are pushing you to do sexual things you don't want to do. What do you do?

a) Put up with it. At least they like you and want to get physical and try things out with you. If you say anything, you'll probably lose them.

b) Suggest other things you could do that wouldn't make you feel uncomfortable. You don't want to be seen as a prude, after all.

c) Tell your partner firmly that you don't want to do those things. A relationship is a two-way thing, and you're saying "no". End of.

Turn the page to see what your answers reveal...

What do my answers mean?

These were tricky questions and there's no simple answer to any of them, but if you chose the **a)** answers, perhaps it's time to think about your relationship values and how much you're willing to stick to them. If you went for the **b)**s, you're aware of what's not right, but you're not really solving things, are you? The **c)** options are the bravest, most honest options, but they're far from easy ones. Good luck!

Chapter Fourteen

What makes you feel good?

What would your answer be to that question? Perhaps something like 'having lots of great mates', 'my team winning a match' or 'getting good grades at school'. Those are all perfectly good answers, but perhaps the best, most *inclusive*, response would include all these things (and a few more):

I feel at my best when I'm HAPPY and HEALTHY.

Happy and healthy. You'll often see these two words together, as a pair. You'll have seen them quite a few times in this book, and that's because, when talking about how people feel, it's pretty clear that you need BOTH to feel really good.

Hopefully, you're now full of ideas for how to *move more* and *eat well*, so the 'healthy' part of your life is getting there. But what about the 'happy' part? Well, this chapter suggests ways of helping yourself feel great in what many experts say is the best way possible, by:

Doing something worthwhile

Meaningful stuff

Earlier, you made a list of what makes you feel good (and some of the things that get you down) but research shows that what makes us happiest of ALL is something called 'meaningful activity'.

You might think this sounds a bit *serious*, but experts believe that real, long-lasting happiness comes from more than a quick 'boost', which soon wears off and can be disappointing. (Yup, maybe eating that whole jar of peanut butter *wasn't* such a good idea.) Instead, it's something that lasts a lot longer, because it *means* something a) to you, b) to other people or c) to both. It may also tie in with the list of 'things that matter to you' you made earlier in the book.

Turn the page for some feel-good suggestions...

A gift from me to you ♡

Feel-good suggestions

OK, so switch off your '<u>critical voice</u>' and read all these ideas through *slowly and thoughtfully*. They may sound simple enough, but any of these suggestions can spark a real sense of wellbeing and contentment. Which one do you think might do that for you?

1 Make time to catch up with a mate you haven't been in touch with for a while. Ask them how they're doing, and tell them (fairly briefly) how things are for you.

Hi there!

Buddy, it's been too long.

2 Cook or bake a treat for someone who you think needs a bit of a boost. If you can, stay for a chat or share it with them when you deliver it.

I know it isn't your birthday, but cake can sometimes be a good idea.

3 Ask at home if there are any unused items you can upcycle. Sand them, paint them, stick on some photos or pictures. Be creative, use your imagination and make it your own. Anything goes, really.

231

4 Sort through your wardrobe, and sell or donate things you don't need and/or won't wear again. If you sell stuff, that can fund your next purchase. Result!

STUFF TO SELL

5 Commit to helping others for a day. Say a cheery "hello", open doors for people, help parents or carers struggling with buggies. Small things, but they can mean a lot.

After you!

6 Plant some seeds in a pot, seedlings in a window box or tomato plants in a hanging basket. Now water and nurture them and wait for a lasting sense of achievement. You may not grow prize-winning vegetables, but nothing beats sharing something you have grown yourself.

Help yourself

7 Try something completely new. Learn to salsa from an online demo; perfect the downward dog; stand on one leg to clean your teeth; listen to some totally new music. Expand your boundaries a little!

Part of the community

There's another factor that influences how good we feel: **other people.** In today's digital world, people can feel isolated from the community they live in. Experts say that loneliness can cause enormous unhappiness, and even illness. Some fear that a sense of community, of everyone needing and supporting each other, is being lost. Why not make it your mission to do *a few small things to restore it where you live?*

Here are a few ideas to get you involved with the people around you. They may take you out of your comfort zone at first, but they will make you feel pretty good, and may help someone else feel even better.

There must be someone who could use our help today.

1) Arrange to watch a movie you love with someone you know who might like it too. The choice is yours, but the main thing is to enjoy spending time together watching it. ☑

2) Do a paper round. You'll earn a bit of cash, get to know who lives in your neighbourhood and become a small part of their daily routine. A cheery wave can go a long way... ☐

3) Elderly people can be especially lonely. Can you commit to popping in to chat, mow their lawn or weed the garden of a elderly person occasionally? ☐

4) Instead of just following groups on social media, find out about some in your area and JOIN them. You don't need to commit to running a pop-up café, but perhaps you can get involved in your community in some way? ☐

Don't say "no", say "YES"!

This idea might feel a bit weird, but it may give you a feel-good boost when you least expect it. The basic approach is a simple one: instead of instantly saying "no", why not say "yes" to new experiences or opportunities.

Be sensible, of course. Do NOT say "yes" to abseiling without a rope or jumping into a pool if you can't swim, BUT adopting a more positive, accepting attitude to what life offers you can be a *really good thing*.

This might take some getting used to, as it may feel unfamiliar to start with, but try to adopt a measured, calm approach to new suggestions:

- **Listen carefully to the opportunity being offered. It could be something like "Do you want to go bowling on Saturday?".**
- **Be aware of your inner, negative voice. It might already be saying: "I can't/I'll be rubbish/No way".**
- **Try to shut that voice down and say: "Sure, I'll give it a go/Why not?".**
- **Go along, and don't spoil it by fretting about what others think of you.**
- **Congratulate yourself if you went against any anxious, cautious 'no-saying' instincts and did something new. Go you!**

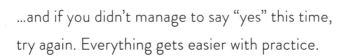

...and if you didn't manage to say "yes" this time, try again. Everything gets easier with practice.

Face your fear

In our need only to do things that make us feel good, it's easy to avoid new, or potentially challenging experiences in case they might make us feel anxious. Some teens feel they can't go on public transport, and others are excused from answering questions in class in case it triggers their anxiety, for example. This is better than ignoring these very real issues, but avoidance can make anxiety worse if you never, ever do something that worries you even a bit. It all comes back to that vital word:

BALANCE

It's always pretty tricky to get the balance right.

Sadly, life is rarely a smooth ride. Everyone has happy times, and not so happy times. Some things make us feel good, but others don't. Good mental health is important, but by never doing anything that may be uncomfortable, some believe young people are ill-equipped for life, with its many ups and downs. By not facing these things, they are not building up their reserves of that key life skill – resilience, or inner toughness.*

Maybe I'll be braver today.

Everyone meets challenges in life, but **it's how you deal with them that counts.** If you hide from anything that's out of your comfort zone, you'll never develop that protective outer shell that we all need – and that could leave you feeling very miserable indeed. Remember, when things get tough, you're not alone, because:

<u>Nobody</u> feels good, <u>all</u> the time.

*See Chapter 8 for lots more about resilience.

You can do this

Next time you face something that makes you want to run for the hills, try to take a moment, a few deep breaths and ask yourself:

"I don't want to do this... but how happy will I feel if I try?"

You know the answer to that, don't you? You'll feel FAB. And even if you can't do it, be proud that you were brave enough to *try*.

Next time, you never know...

I need to believe in myself. I CAN do this.

Can you make a list of some things that you know you would find a bit tricky? They might include going into school with a new haircut, telling a mate you can't make their party or telling a teacher you don't understand the task.

How might you be able to tackle the things on your list in a mature, resilient way, so that they become worry-free zones? You might try:

* Reminding yourself that EVERYONE has things they find tricky at times.
* Telling yourself that you CAN and WILL do this and shutting down your doubts.
* Remembering that this is YOUR choice. No one can make you do things you don't want to do.

YOU'VE GOT THIS

Experiences that challenge you are an investment in the growth of the positive, healthy, STRONG person you want to become. You'll increase your levels of self-esteem and learn a lot about yourself as well. Remember the old cliché: *nothing ventured, nothing gained.*

What kind of person are you?

Choose one answer for each of these questions:

Q1: You've had a message from someone you really liked who moved away a few years ago. They want to hear from you. What do you do?

a)   Delete the message. It's been too long and you're probably totally different people now.

b)   Send a friendly, but brief, message outlining what you're doing and asking after them and their family.

c)   Say how good it is to hear from them and suggest a meeting if they are ever in the area. It would be good to know how they are.

Q2: An elderly neighbour hasn't taken their bins in this week. Usually, they do so straightaway. What do you do?

a)   Nothing. It's up to their family to check up on them, not you.

b)   Pop a note through the door, asking if they're OK. Tell them you live nearby, but don't give too many personal details, just in case.

c)   Go with a parent or carer to call on them. If they don't answer the door, discuss with your adult what's best to do next.

Q3: You're feeling frustrated and bored, because none of your group of friends seems to want to *do* anything very much. What do you do?

a) Go with the flow. Load up another game and hope somebody has a fun idea before the weekend.

b) Research some local clubs, classes or groups online, and make a list of possibilities to suggest to them. It's a start, anyway.

c) Decide what you're interested in, and find out what's going on in your area that you could try by yourself (and maybe meet new people).

Q4: A friend has offered you a ticket to go with them to see a DJ that you've never heard of. What do you do?

a) Say "Thanks, but no thanks." If you haven't even heard of the DJ, they can't be any good.

b) Check the DJ out, listen to some of their stuff and research the sort of people who like them. If you're still not sure, say you'd rather not.

c) Accept and see what happens. Any live music is a good experience, so think positive and go with your mate to find out more.

Turn the page to see what your answers reveal...

What do my answers mean?

Once again, there are no 'right' answers of course, but there are ones that *could* make you feel good, and ones that definitely *won't*. If you chose the **a)** answers, perhaps you need to be a bit more open-minded in terms of what could make you happy. If you went for the **b)**s, you're dipping your toe in the water, which is good, but the **c)** answers help you actually *commit* to doing things that could enrich your life. Why not think positively, and take a chance?

Chapter Fifteen

Teen survival tips

In this final chapter, you'll find some of the advice you've read so far in each section summed-up in five handy 'survival tips'.

They aim to give you some clear pointers, and mean you won't have to look back through each chapter to find guidance if you need it fast.

It helps to know where to look, fast, to get some advice.

Hopefully, these tips will be useful as you navigate some of the many challenges these teenage years can bring.

Because let's face it:

There are strong emotions, seriously-swinging moods and plenty of school-based stress in the mix. Add spots, your changing body, <u>FOMO</u> (fear of missing out) and perfect-looking celebs all over social media, and things can feel very pressured indeed. No, it's not an easy time...

but it is an  one.

These are the years when you are gradually becoming your grown-up self, an important member of society and a young adult with thoughts, ideas and values of your own. Along the way, you are bound to encounter people you don't get on with, or people who don't look at things the way you do. That's life and it's OK.

One of the biggest problems teens encounter is how to respond and react to others around them, because their emotions are often in overdrive. If you lose your temper, it's hard to come back from that and confrontation with your family or friends is upsetting. If you can, try to be considerate and patient in how you respond to others. Bascially, everyone wants an easy life, so go with the flow as much as possible.

Aim to be the bigger person, and decide to try not to lose it with those around you.

1 Managing your moods

OK, so everyone knows teens are moody: they have bad moods, confusing moods, dark moods, ones that arrive for no particular reason and won't go away and ones that make them feel that *nobody understands them AT ALL*. If you're struggling to manage *your* moods, here are some ways of defusing a potential 'explosion':

* Breathe deeply and focus ONLY on your breathing for a few minutes, slowly in ...and out, in ...and out. The rage will pass.

* Walk away before you say that really horrible thing that's on the tip of your tongue and that you may well regret saying later.

* Think before you speak Close your eyes and count to ten in your head. This buys time to cool down.

* Focus on your surroundings, not your feelings Looking outside yourself can help 'ground' you again. Choose a particular object, and focus on it.

* Step away, and **write your feelings down or record saying them on your phone** to regain some control. It can really help, honestly.

...and if none of these things works and you DO explode, when you have calmed down...

* Say sorry, and mean it Friends and family will usually forgive and forget, but you need to remember it's hard for them too when you say horrible things. Work on managing your emotions better next time.

② Doing stuff

It's easy to get bogged down in the everyday routine of school and work and stop doing the things you know make you feel good. If you find yourself feeling a bit low and lacking 'oomph' from time to time, try these tips:

* **Get outside and into the fresh air**
  A ten minute walk is often enough to clear your head and cheer you up.

* **Do something with other people**
  Play a game, kick a ball, walk a dog, meet mates at the shops...

One class goal coming up...

* Organize something to look forward to
Arrange to see a friend, plan a trip out or book a ticket for a gig. It gives you something to look forward to.

* Do something you find relaxing to recharge your batteries. Play a game, watch a movie or do some cooking. The choice is yours.

* Give yourself a treat It could be a sugary, fatty or salty one, but that's absolutely fine every now and then – just not too often, OK?

...and if none of these tips helps, **tell yourself that *"tomorrow is another day"*** (because it is) and will be better (because it might well be).

That was one tough day. Bring on tomorrow!

It may sound weird, but **accepting *who* you are and *how* you are** is a key part of being happy. It's not easy, especially at your age, as everything can feel against you at times, but try these tips:

* **Make a quick list of three things you like about yourself** Nobody else needs to see it, but it may help if you write it down or type it.

* Say to yourself (out loud if you wish):

> **NOBODY is perfect.**

This is 100% true, folks. Just sayin'.

* **Jot down three things you are good at**
They can be simple stuff, like
I make a mean cheese toastie.
But that's fine.

* Shut down the negative voice in your head
as soon as you notice it. It won't help you, and it often tells lies.

You're no good.

Listen up. I'M in charge here, NOT you.

* Think about the people that love you
Sure, you have faults, but they still care about you and how you're doing, don't they? You can't be all bad.

...and if these don't help, remember:

I'm just as good as anyone else and I am worthy of kindness and respect.

Because YOU ARE.

As a teen, your family (be it parents, carers and/or siblings) can cause you a huge amount of stress. You may feel as if they make your life much more difficult, and don't 'get' you AT ALL. If this is you, these tips might help:

* **Having disagreements with those close to you is normal right now** You're 'flexing your new adult muscles' and they're not used to it.

* When you argue, **reflect** on it. Could you have been more patient, or understanding? That's how you'll **learn to do things better next time.**

* **Your family are not mind-readers** Talk to them, tell them how you feel and what you need from them right now. It's a good start anyway.

Need a hug?

Oh Gran, I'm so confused. Can we talk?

* **Use different tactics** If yelling at your family isn't working (clue: it rarely does) try writing what you need to say in a clear email, text or note.

* **Accept reality** Your family are a bit like 'the friends you didn't choose'. They will always be in your life, and you'll have good, and bad times together.

...and if none of these helps, **ask your mates if they sometimes struggle with their families.** Bet they do. It happens: always has, and always will.

⑤ Friendship problems

Friends are important to everyone, but friendships during your teenage years can be intense, and that may lead to problems at times. Here are some sound tips for surviving them:

* Choose your friends wisely Look for people who enjoy the things you do and share your values and priorities in life. That's a solid foundation to build on.

* Treat your friends as you'd like them to treat you Sounds simple, but doing this cuts out a pile of negative possibilities.

* Friends have their own lives, and worries, so **try not to expect too much of them** as you may end up disappointed.

> Sia's late, but I know she's busy.

* Give people a second chance

If you fall out with a friend, see if you can find a way to fix things. We *all* make mistakes, don't we?

* Be true to you

If friends are doing something you disagree with, you don't have to join them. A real friend wouldn't ask you to.

...and if none of these helps, **remember that you'll have LOTS of friendships during your life** – not all of them will last forever, but some just might.

Remember when we met in high school?

SNAP

Seems a lifetime ago – probably because it is!

There are several chapters in this book all about how to be as healthy as you can be. Here are the take-away (haha) food tips to bear in mind as you live your busy life:

* Eat food that's GOOD for your body
Well, you only get one and you want it to last, don't you?

* You are designed to move, so **do something active as often as you can,** something that gets your body moving and the blood pumping.

Woohoo!

I love coming here after school.

* Accept that no two human bodies are the same They come in many, many, MANY different shapes and sizes – including yours.

* Think of food, water and sleep as essential fuel for your body
Without enough of them, you won't run well and may 'break down' (in other words, 'get ill'!).

* Have, and enjoy, treats from time to time It's good to eat healthily, but it's also important to treat yourself a bit too, without guilt or regret.

...and if none of these tips helps, get a mate on board and work out a fun, realistic health and fitness plan to stick to, together.

Let's do this...

Together!

7 Mental wellbeing

HANDLE WITH CARE

FRAGILE

Mental health is an important issue for everyone. Here are some tips for taking care of your mental health if things get tough:

* **Remember that you are not alone**
  Everyone feels anxious or panicky from time to time, because life can sometimes be really stressful.

* **Get to know your body** Then, you'll recognize the physical signs of anxiety in time to respond rather than react, giving the feeling of anxiety time to ease off.

If I feel anxious, I do some painting, to feel calmer.

* However powerful your feelings may be, **feelings are NOT facts.** They will change, and even vanish, in time. Hold onto that 100% real fact until they do.

* If you're struggling with school pressures, **remember that all you can do is your best.** Do that, and then feel happy with yourself. End of.

* Be kind to YOU

These years are a rollercoaster ride, with lots of ups and downs. Be kind to yourself and to others, and hold on tight.

...and if none of these tips helps, or you're worried about something, **ask for support.** Everyone needs help at times.

If you do need help, you can find out more about some mental health issues that might affect you at **Usborne Quicklinks**.

Young people are probably the biggest users of social media, in all its forms. It can be a great thing... and a not-so-great thing, too. Bear these tips in mind to keep all those 'socials' in control:

* The online world is NOT the real world
The information and photos you see there may not be 'real' either. Don't always believe what you see.

* Use social media for good in your life
Stay in touch with friends, find things out, join groups, enjoy funny memes. We all need a laugh!

* Remember that whatever you post or comment is there forever This may help you think twice before pressing that button.

* Nothing can replace face-to-face contact with a person Make time for real, live people as well as spending it scrolling and posting.

* Be aware of how much time you're spending on social media. **Stay in control,** so that it's a part of your life, but far from all of it.

...and if none of these tips feels do-able, it might be time to look at cutting back on your social media activity for a while. Just a thought.

9 Money management

Managing your money well is a habit worth learning *now*, so that you'll have it for life. Here are some tips to bear in mind as you learn how to keep in control of money:

Right, budget! Let's get you under control.

* **Before you buy something, think is it a 'need' or a 'want'?** This should stop you buying your sixth pair of white trainers.

* Don't spend what you don't have. Simple, but true. **If you can't pay for it, don't buy it.**

* **Be aware of others** who may not have as much money as you, or your family do. Be sensitive, aware of different circumstances and kind, always.

* Remember that (hopefully) your parents or carers pay for you to be safe, warm, fed and dressed. Try to **be grateful!** You know you can...

* Some of the best things in life are free
Really, they are. If you aim just to have fun with friends or family, it will probably mean more if you haven't blown the budget.

And a final tip: remember to **keep track of what money comes in, and what's going out.** Balance that budget!*

⑩ The relationship minefield

These years will be full of relationships with people. Some will be straightforward, some amazing, but some might be a steep learning curve. Here are some basic tips to help you steer a steady course:

* **Value and respect yourself** If anyone, in any relationship in your life, doesn't value and respect you, it's time to stand up for yourself, and perhaps move on.

* **Expect the unexpected** This is new territory, as your body, your brain and your feelings are changing rapidly, and there are no instructions.

* **Accept things may go wrong, and you may get hurt emotionally** This is how you'll develop resilience, even though it's difficult at the time.

* Be open-minded and accepting of others

Treat other people with respect, however different you are. You might learn a lot from someone *who's unlike* you.

* You are still changing and developing

Don't feel pressured to fit into a certain mould.
You are you, whoever you end up being.

...and last of all, remember that **a relationship is, at its heart, a connection with another person,** and can come in many, many different forms.

And finally...

Hopefully, you've found this book full of useful stuff about some of the things you'll encounter during this time in your life. No two teens will be the same, or experience the same thoughts, feelings or problems, but *all* of them will face challenges in some form. That's a dead cert.

Despite this, try to remember that this is an EXCITING time, full of things to try, find out about, learn and cherish. This chapter has lots of lists, but here's one *final* list for you. Let's call it the 'tips for living your best life' list. If you can, bear them in mind – and enjoy the ride!

1. Live your values

Now's the time you'll begin to think about what matters to you, and what things you feel strongly about. Try to include them in your your life: you could volunteer, sign petitions, campaign, join groups, protest or simply help others in small ways.

2. Accept and adapt

Life is rarely (well, never) exactly how you want it to be. If you can, strive to accept what you have and adapt to things you have to get used to. This doesn't mean you can't hope for better. It means you just don't expect perfection, from anything or anyone.

3. Be your best self

This does NOT mean you can never be scared, sad, angry or grumpy at times, because you will be, and that's OK. Surviving the teenage years is tricky, but you will. Simply aim to be true to yourself, a genuine, kind, but imperfect human being. That's enough.

You've got this.

Glossary

addiction
an illness which means you are unable to stop doing something which may be harming you

additives
chemicals sometimes added to food

adrenaline
a hormone released by the body which makes you feel excited, breathe more quickly and gets your muscles ready for exercise

amygdala
a small part of the brain that influences how we experience and express emotions

anorexia nervosa
an illness which makes people believe that they need to lose weight when they don't

anxiety
a feeling of fear, panic and worry

app (application)
software designed to run on a mobile device

body positivity
a movement that encourages people to be happy with their bodies

budgeting
controlling your money so that you don't spend more than you have

bulimia
an illness in which people make themselves vomit after eating as they fear putting on any weight

bullying
deliberate, repeated abuse by a powerful person of a less powerful one

climate change
long-term shifts in temperature and weather patterns around the world

consent
agreement to something that is about to happen

cortisol
a chemical the brain produces when you are scared or stressed

critical voice
an imagined voice in your head that criticizes you and makes you feel bad

depression
an illness which makes people very unhappy, tired and unable to enjoy life

diet[1]
the food you eat

diet[2]
restrictions that limit what you eat, often to lose or gain weight

endorphins
chemicals released by the brain that can make you feel happier

expenses
amounts of money you need to spend on things you have to pay for

flexitarian
someone who mainly
follows a vegetarian
diet, but sometimes
eats meat and fish

FOMO
a feeling, known as the
'Fear Of Missing Out'

gender
what sex you are

gender identity
your sense of what sex
you feel yourself to be

hikikomori
a Japanese word for
a young person who
feels they cannot be
with other people, and
is often online 24/7

hormones
chemicals the body
produces to tell it
what to do and when
to do it

hypertense
very stressed and on
edge all the time

income
how much money you
earn, or have coming in

melatonin
a chemical the body
produces to help
prepare it for sleep

mental health
how we feel and how
we cope when faced
with the challenges
life brings

notification
an alert telling you
of a new message,
post or update online

peer
someone who is about
the same age and in
the same situation
in life as you are

porn (pornography)
staged images of sexual
activity that aim to
excite people sexually

puberty
the years during
which children begin
to mature into adults

resilience
inner strength, or
toughness, which gets you
through difficult times

self-esteem
confidence in and
valuing yourself

sexism
treating people of
a particular sex in a
discriminatory way

sexuality
a person's identity in
relation to the gender
or genders to which
they are attracted

social media
online sites and apps
that you can use to
share pictures and ideas
or contact people

stereotype
a very limited idea
of what any kind
of person is like

stress
the body's reaction
to sensing fear
or danger

toxic masculinity
an attitude to women
that sees them as
inferior to men

vegan
someone who does not
eat anything that has
come from an animal

vegetarian
someone who does not
eat any meat or fish

Index

A

B

C

Cover design by
Matthew Durber

First published in 2024 by Usborne Publishing Limited,
83-85 Saffron Hill, London EC1N 8RT, United Kingdom.

usborne.com

Printed in the UK. UKE.